From The Bronx To Berchtesgaden

The Combat Memoir
Of a World War II Hero

By Murray Soskil
3rd Infantry Division

Temurlone Press • New York

Published by
Temurlone Press
www.temurlonepress.com

Copyright © 2012 by Murray Soskil

This is a memoir. As such, it is an account of the recollections of the author. Any errors in fact result from the imperfection of human memory after a sixty-year interval. The opinions expressed herein belong to the author alone.

All rights reserved. No part of this book may be reproduced or transmitted in any form or by any means, electronic or mechanical, including photocopying, recording, or by any information storage-and-retrieval system, without the written permission of the Publisher, except where permitted by law.

Cover design by Gail P. Dubov.

ISBN-10: 0983611734
ISBN-13: 978-0-9836117-3-8

Dogface Soldier
Official Song of the 3rd Division

I Wouldn't Give A Bean
To Be A Fancy Pants Marine,
I'd rather Be A Dogface Soldier Like I Am.

I Wouldn't Trade My Old O.D.'s
For All The Navy's Dungarees
For I'm The Walking Pride Of Uncle Sam;

On All The Posters That I Read
It Says The Army Builds Men
So They're Tearing Me Down To Build Me Over Again

I'm Just A Dogface Soldier
With A Rifle On My Shoulder
And I Eat A Kraut For Breakfast Everyday.

So Feed Me Ammunition,
Keep Me In The Third Division,
Your Dogfaced Soldier Boy's Okay.

— Cpl. Bert Gold and Lt. Ken Hart

Contents

Acknowledgements i
Preface v
The Bronx 1
Basic Training... 7
Shipping Out 19
Warminster.. 27
Invasion 33
Sergeant Soskil 43
Silver Star 55
Across the Moselle 69
Germany.. 85
Operation Krautbuster 99
The Rhine... 119
Arbeit Macht Frei 131
Berchtesgaden 143
Peace... 157
Coming Home 169

Acknowledgements

I kept a journal during combat and jotted down my experiences when I had time to do so between battles. These notes came in handy after I was discharged and settled at home again, when I decided to write an account of my service in the infantry. Words came to me quickly. Soon I had finished fifty pages. Then we were occupied with a special event, the birth of my first son. So my story was put on hold and set aside for six decades.

Some years ago my family was invited to the dedication ceremony in Washington, D.C. for a memorial monument honoring the four hundred thousand service men killed during the Second World War. My wife and I, two of my grandsons, and two of my great-grandsons decided to attend.

From The Bronx to Berchtesgaden

At the memorial my grandson typed my name into a computer and my picture came up with a list of my citations. Everyone was excited. Many people came over to see what was going on. Several said that to meet a live hero some sixty-odd years later made the day memorable for them.

Eventually, the urging of my four older grandsons, Mathew, Michael, Eric, and Brett, and of my granddaughter, Katelyn, who kept saying, "Poppy, can you tell me some of your war stories?", convinced me that I should tell of my experiences. I decided to write this memoir in order to let my children and grandchildren know what it was like being a dogface infantry soldier on the ground in France and Germany during the Second World War.

I went into the attic and dug out the chest that contained my war trophies, pictures, and the notes that I made in combat, including the fifty pages I had started more than sixty years before. I also discovered the letters I had written to my wife, and some of the thousand letters she had written to me while I was overseas.

Most infantrymen had little idea of where they were fighting. One town in a foreign country

Acknowledgements

was very much like every other. The name of the last place where you fought, if you ever knew it, was forgotten the moment your next battle began. I was no exception to this rule. Thus, after the war, I had to refer to such books as *The History of the 3rd Infantry Division* and *The Story of the Blue Devils* in order to identify the route of my division and where we had gone to war.

My army buddy, Seymour Rosen, was helpful in reminding me of incidents I had forgotten. I must thank my daughter-in-law, Carol, who typed the first draft of this manuscript. I must also thank my granddaughter, Jessica, known to us all as the "Princess", who spent hours retyping every time new thoughts came into my mind. I am eternally grateful to my wife, Pearl, for putting up with me throughout the process of writing, and to my son, Marvin, for editing and compiling the final results.

My family, I love you all.

I dedicate this book to my comrades, both those who are still alive and those who paid the highest price.

The surviving veterans of World War II are dying off at the rate of thirty thousand a year. They should always be remembered and honored for their sacrifices.

In war there are no winners. Only losers.

Preface

It was our 65th anniversary. My wife, Pearl, was at my side and we were celebrating with our entire family at the Swan Club in Long Island, New York. This was where we celebrated our 50th anniversary, then our 60th, and now we had the good fortune of celebrating our 65th together. Forty-two of our closest relatives and friends had joined us. As we looked around, we saw the results of our marriage—our three sons, Norman, Marvin, and Joel, with their wives, ten grandchildren, and ten great grandchildren. I could not but help think that there must have been a master plan that kept me alive throughout the war and brought me home to my wife with a sound mind and body, so that I could create my own "Tree of Life."

From The Bronx to Berchtesgaden

A great man, my father, once said, "I look at my family and although I don't have much money, I feel like a billionaire. I am a short man but when I look at my family, I feel ten feet tall."

I now understood his feelings. My only regret was that my parents were not there to see the wonderful Soskil clan that they had started.

The Bronx

I was born May 8, 1922 on the Lower East Side of Manhattan and brought up in The Bronx by a wonderful, hard-working mother and father. There wasn't much money but we always had good food to eat, clean clothes to wear, and plenty of love. I had an older sister, Irene, and another sister was soon on the way. Irene and Selma were two of the most devoted and loving sisters anyone could have.

Our family moved quite often from apartment to apartment so that we could avoid painting and in order to receive free concessions of rent from our new landlords, who would often waive our first month's payment as an inducement to move in.

Most of my youth was spent on Longfellow Avenue in The Bronx. We didn't have much

From The Bronx to Berchtesgaden

athletic equipment, so our games were mainly stickball, kick the can, and Johnny on the pony.

As I grew up, my ritual on Friday after school was to wash the kitchen floor. Then my mother would cover it with newspaper to keep it clean until the next washing. Every other week I would sit on the outside windowsill of our fifth-floor apartment and wash the windows. My sisters held my feet to make sure I wouldn't fall. Each week after my father was paid, he would buy a 5-cent bar of candy and cut it into sections, so each one of us would get a piece. This was a reward for doing our chores. We did not have air conditioning so during the hot summer months we slept on the fire escape. During the summer days we sunned ourselves on the roof, which was known as "Tar Beach", and ran around under open fire hydrants to cool down and escape the heat.

I graduated from James Monroe High School in June, 1938 at the age of sixteen. Because I had been allowed to skip two grades, this happened to be the same day that my older sister Irene graduated. My folks wanted me to go to New York University to become a dentist. However, I knew they could not afford the tuition, so I enrolled in night

The Bronx

school at the City College of New York. During the day I worked in an importing house dealing in watch materials. My salary was $16 per week.

At first my hours were nine to five on weekdays and nine to three on Saturdays. After one year, however, a law was passed limiting full-time employment without overtime to forty hours per week. Since my employers did not want to pay me overtime, my hours were cut and I had both Saturday and Sunday off. My weekday schedule was to leave the house at 8 AM to catch the Freeman Street express train to City Hall Station, and to be in the office at 9 AM. At five o'clock I would eat a sandwich and attend school on 23rd Street from 6 PM to 9 PM. This was my routine for four years with the week of July 4th off for vacation.

For fun I got together with some of my buddies and we formed a "cellar club", which we called *Palladium*. The club room was located in the basement of a rabbi's house. It had nine couches, some donated and others bought second-hand. There was a record player and plenty of records. The ceiling was decorated with phosphorous stars. The strategic placement of dim lighting created quite a romantic ambiance.

From The Bronx to Berchtesgaden

Since there were many similar cellar clubs in the neighborhood, we needed a gimmick in order to attract girls to our place. So we rented a room in a temple nearby and invited the parents of all the girls we knew. We asked each set of parents to bring a dish of their specialty food. We supplied the entertainment. The boys were on their best behavior, which impressed the mothers, and instead of trying to keep their daughters away from us, they encouraged them to go meet the *nice boys*. On Friday nights, with only fifteen male members in the club, an average of thirty girls came by. It was hectic trying to entertain them all.

One of my club members was Sydney Zeidman. We were best friends together in kindergarten through high school and remained friends for seventy years until he died of a heart attack.

At the time I was seeing a girl named Sadie. She lived in the West Bronx. I got there on a crosstown bus. It would make its last run at 2:30 AM and somehow I always missed it, so I would get home pretty late. My mother did not like Sadie, who smoked cigarettes. Mom told me to find a girl in the East Bronx. Fortunately, I did.

The Bronx

The Palladium had quite an influence on my life. It was where I met the girl of my dreams. One of our steadies brought a girl named Pearl down to the club. She was to be a blind date for one of the boys. She did not know who she was meant to be with and I convinced her that she was supposed to be with me. We danced together most of the evening even though I had hurt my foot that afternoon. It was strange, but although I couldn't walk, I was able to dance for hours.

Somehow I knew immediately that Pearl was the girl for me. I wanted to walk her home but because of my leg injury I wasn't able to. Pearl offered me her bus transfers so that I could take the bus and she walked home with some other boys. Luckily, I must have made a good impression on her, because she soon became my girl. We started going steady and a year later we became engaged.

At the time I was making $29 a week. Pearl was talking of marriage but I felt we had to wait until I was making at least $35.

I was happy in spite of my busy schedule of work and school. I had a job that covered my expenses and a fiancé who was the most beautiful girl

From The Bronx to Berchtesgaden

I had ever seen. An added bonus was that Pearl was liked by everyone, even my mother, who liked her because she lived nearby, which gave me no excuse to come home late. My father, of course, took to Pearl at once. Life was going well—until December 7, 1941. Pearl Harbor.

Basic Training

Soon the Palladium was closed and the cellar club was disbanded. Ten of the fellows left for the service. Two were given 4-F ratings and three went to work in defense plants. Since I had experience in a watch-importing plant, and knew how to use fine measuring instruments, it was easy for me to get placed in a defense plant, too. My job was making dies for shells. I started to earn $80 a week plus overtime. With all that income, I was comfortable enough to go along with plans for a wedding. Pearl and I started making arrangements and we set the date for Saturday, April 10th.

Two deferments later, I received a notice to appear for induction on Monday, April 12, 1942, two days after our wedding. On the Friday before the wedding, I got a notice giving me an additional thirty-day deferment. This allowed the wedding to be a little more festive than it would have been.

My sister Irene had a boyfriend who was already in the service. He was in the Coast Guard and stationed permanently at Sheepshead Bay in Brooklyn. One day he informed me that the Coast Guard was looking for typists. If I could get a permanent position at the base, I would not have to go overseas. Even better, I would be able to see my wife almost every night. Although I had never typed before, I went out and bought a typewriter. All night long I tried to teach myself how to type.

The next day I went to the Coast Guard for the test. They gave me a long sheet of paper, which I had to type in ten minutes. After five minutes I was a third of the way through and my work was peppered with mistakes.

My friend Marvin came over and sat down in my place and finished the rest of the test for me. When I turned in the paper, the chief commented that I must have been nervous in the beginning, referring to my mistakes, but that my accuracy had improved as I calmed down. Then he sent me back

Basic Training

to my draft board to get permission to join the Coast Guard. They, in turn, sent me back to the Coast Guard to get a request form. Before I could turn this in, however, I received a notice to appear for induction into the U.S. Army. It was too late to join the Coast Guard.

Pearl and I had a wonderful two-day honeymoon in the Victoria Hotel on Broadway in New York City. Somehow we found time to go to the circus and to have a great dinner at a restaurant called Toffenetti's. Then it was back to work the following morning. And just a month later, after many tearful good-byes with Pearl, I left for the induction center on Arthur Avenue in The Bronx, where I was sworn in and immediately shipped out to Camp Schenango in western Pennsylvania.

The army wasted no time processing new recruits. We were herded into a large building and told to strip off our clothes and to line up. Modesty was not permitted. Being stark naked with a group of naked strangers was not a comfortable experience. Some men were tense and embarrassed. When someone laughed, everyone laughed.

There was a line of booths, each containing a

From The Bronx to Berchtesgaden

group of doctors with a different specialty, and we were instructed to pass from one booth to another. At each stop we received an examination. We were checked from head to toe. We stood around naked to receive short-arm inspections and all types of injections. After what seemed like hours we were given GI uniforms but few men were provided with uniforms that fit although later on we were able to trade with each other until we all had clothes the right size. Next we were herded to a line of barber chairs, each with a barber beside it. These barbers had only one thing in mind, which was to shave you bald. They did not ask how you wanted your hair styled. Off it came, completely.

Finally we were ordered into another room, which was decorated with a big American flag, where an officer formally swore us in to the United States Army. We were a bunch of frightened, bewildered, and lonely young men.

We were no longer civilians but soldiers in the U.S. Army. There were forms to fill out, payroll books to receive, dog tags to hang around your neck, and insurance applications to complete. There were many injections to be had, including typhoid and

Basic Training

tetanus. We were given the Soldier's Handbook to memorize in two days. It contained the General Orders. We had to know this material in case we were stopped and drilled by noncoms or officers. When I was not doing close-order drills, or picking up trash, a task known as *policing*, I spent my time studying the General Orders and writing letters home. I learned a strange army expression: *The eating place was a mess and the sleeping place was a bunk.*

The barracks to which I was assigned had two-tier bunk beds on opposite sides of the room. I was in an upper bunk. The first couple nights I couldn't sleep for fear of falling off the bed. The strange noises didn't help. I could hear some men crying from fright and loneliness while others were just snoring away. I eventually fell asleep dreaming of home.

It wasn't long before I received my assignment. I was to take my training in the Aberdeen Proving Grounds, which was an Ordinance camp. We boarded the train in daylight and rolled into camp in the middle of the night. Drill sergeants led us to our barracks. Our drill sergeant showed us who was boss right from the beginning. He was tough and he had a pronounced hillbilly accent.

From The Bronx to Berchtesgaden

The second day at camp there was some confusion in the ranks. Some of the guys screwed up. They were late for inspection. At morning formation our sergeant showed us what happened if we were not all in unison. He scheduled us with two hours of close order drill for Saturday.

At first glance the camp looked like a country club. It had four movie houses, a swimming pool, and a lake with rowboats. But it was not fun at all. There was plenty of sweat and long hours of training. The daily routine began at 6 AM, when a corporal came through the barracks and got everyone out of bed. We washed, shaved, dressed in fatigues and plastic helmet liners, and made our beds. The blanket had to be tucked as tight and smooth as possible. When these chores were done, it was time to fall in for reveille and the raising of the flag. Then we ate breakfast and returned to the barracks to get ready for the day's activities.

In addition to my basic training, I learned how to repair range finders, binoculars, and other fine control instruments.

We had endless bayonet drills, rifle practice, and field marches in full kits, pounding at a breathless

Basic Training

pace. Each day we started with a five-mile hike that must be completed in one hour. There was no trotting or running allowed, just a fast walk. The first time, only 10 out of 180 finished in time. After a few weeks, 90 percent of the company made it. We also had to contend with guard duty, plenty of GI parties, and KP. At night I had no trouble sleeping. Besides being tired, I wanted to start dreaming of being home with my wife. Whenever I got the chance, I would wait in line for hours just to make a phone call home.

My buddies in Aberdeen included Bob Stern, who worked in a jewelry store with his father; Joe Campella, who worked for the Post Office; Stan Axelrod, who was a college student; and Sid Stone, who worked with his father in a plumbing-supply business. They were all helpful to me in getting passes when Pearl visited Aberdeen. We five went to England together but we were soon separated, except for Sid Stone and I. We joined the 3rd Infantry Division together. Sid was killed his first day in action.

One weekend Pearl showed up with her baggage. She was determined to stay in Aberdeen. That evening we went looking for sleeping accommodations. The only place we could find was a tavern, which we later learned was actually a whorehouse. There was a pot under the bed to be used as a toilet. I moved the dresser behind the door to make sure we did not have visitors.

The next two nights we slept in a motel at the rate of $50 a night. My army pay was $50 a month but we could find nothing else. Outside the camp gates were houses for the personnel working in the Proving Grounds. Pearl went from house to house, trying to rent a room. After being turned down at the last place, Pearl sat on the steps and started to cry. The woman of the house felt sorry for her and said we could stay for the weekend. We ended up staying there the entire time we spent in Aberdeen. With a little extra cash, I managed to get quite a few overnight passes. Love conquered all.

Pearl got a job in the Proving Grounds. Her job allowed her to go anywhere in the camp, including the areas where soldiers were not permitted. One day I received a weekend pass so we decided to visit the folks in New York. We arranged to meet at the camp gate and to take a taxi to the railway station. As I waited at the gate, a car approached. Pearl stuck her head out of the window and waved for me to get

Basic Training

Murray Soskil.

in. As I opened the door, I saw a captain sitting in the back seat. At that time, a captain frightened me as much as a general. When Pearl introduced me, I didn't know whether to salute or shake hands, so I did both. He left us off at the train station.

We made it a habit to call my folks every

From The Bronx to Berchtesgaden

Thursday at a specific time. This particular Thursday all passes were cancelled without notice and we were confined to barracks. There was going to be a special inspection by the colonel of the camp.

Pearl got the news and decided to call my folks so they wouldn't worry. When she spoke to my mother, the first thing out of my mother's mouth was, "Where is Murray?" Pearl told her that I was at a GI party. Mom asked, "So why didn't he take you?"

Another Sunday, when I was on guard duty, Pearl followed our squad to the guardhouse and then followed me to my post. As I walked back and forth, Pearl sat on the grass and fed me cookies and candy. My post was in front of officers' quarters. When an officer came out and started flirting with Pearl, I got so angry, I had a hard time stopping myself from going after him, which was just as well, because I would have been court-martialed.

All too soon basic training was over and it was time for Pearl and I to say our good-byes once again. I was being shipped to Ohio. Pearl told me she was returning to New York. But when our transport train groaned to a stop, Pearl was waiting at the railway station. She had found out from officers at the Proving

Basic Training

Grounds where we were being sent. I couldn't believe she was there. Unfortunately, we were only at this camp a short time, just long enough to get our classifications and a few more injections, but at least Pearl and I had a few more nights together.

Then I was sent to Camp Upton, on Long Island, where we waited to be shipped overseas. The boys were betting that when we got to our destination, wherever in the world we were assigned, Pearl would be there to greet us when we arrived.

At Camp Upton I was promoted to the rank of acting corporal. I was assigned to bring a group of men into Manhattan to become naturalized citizens. The soldier who drove the bus told me to meet him in five hours to return to camp. We were finished in court after two hours so I called Pearl. Perhaps we could grab some time together once more. Since we were in midtown Manhattan, we went to a movie, *Guadalcanal Diary*. When the picture was over, I had only a few minutes to catch the bus back to Upton. I gave Pearl a peck on the cheek, expecting to see her that night on a pass, and ran for the bus. Little did I know that I would not see Pearl again for almost three years.

Shipping Out

Soon after arriving back at camp, we were put on alert. We got our equipment together and that evening we boarded buses that took us to our ship. Boarding with full packs was not an easy task. We climbed ladders to get on deck. We were not told what our destination was going to be but our kits included mosquito netting, so we assumed we were going to the Pacific.

It was not until we were at sea that we were we told our destination was England. We were given instructions on how American servicemen should conduct themselves there. We were warned not to criticize the king or English politics. The first morning as we started out we all went on deck and looked upon at the calm water.

From The Bronx to Berchtesgaden

We saw a convoy of thirty ships of all sizes, from small cruisers to freighters and tankers. The speed of the convoy had to accommodate the slowest vessel. Navy ships accompanied us, but we could not see how many war vessels there were.

Our ship was a French liner with a rounded bottom made for the calm waters of the Mediterranean, not for the North Atlantic in winter. The ship was the *Louis Pasteur*. She was huge, weighed twenty-eight thousand tons, and carried six thousand troops plus a crew of five hundred. Although the *Louis Pasteur* was a French ship, the crew was English. We were put in a large room, which held twenty soldiers. Our beds were hammocks placed close together and interlocking head to feet. When one hammock moved, they all swayed.

As we passed the Statue of Liberty, no one thought that we would be away more than a year, and there were no thoughts of not returning. Dusk was setting in but we still could make out the other ships in the convoy and I was mesmerized by the wake trailing behind the vessels. Looking out over the water was calming but even though there were a thousand men all around me, I felt lonely. I couldn't stop thinking

Shipping Out

The *Louis Pasteur*. Photo from the personal collection of Conrad Byers.

about my family. Then, a few hours out of the harbor, the water started to get rough.

Not only did we go up and down but the ship also rolled from side to side. Swells slammed against the vessel and the waves swept over the deck. We were below being tossed about helplessly as the ship made frequent course changes in order to avoid prowling enemy submarines. I was in no mood for food and I spent much time running from my bunk to the latrine along with most of my companions. Even the crew were moaning and retching.

From The Bronx to Berchtesgaden

It took nine days to cross the ocean. I lost a lot of weight. We arrived at the port of Bristol, England, glad to be on dry land. As we approached the dock, a crowd of people cheered and waved to us. There was a military band playing marches. The boys were all on deck and waving back, throwing packs of cigarettes to the multitudes on the dock. We disembarked and got on to trucks, which took us to our new barracks.

Not long afterward there was a confrontation between some black troops, who had arrived first, and some white paratroopers, who had arrived in England more recently. Apparently the black American soldiers were monopolizing the single Bristol women, which did not sit well with the white paratroopers. There was bloodshed among our own men. All military personnel were prohibited from going into town.

One Friday night a few Jewish soldiers and I were invited to the house of an English Jewish family to share their traditional Sabbath dinner and services. It certainly felt like home with their dinner of *gefilte* fish and brisket of beef. Our hosts were gracious. We could not thank them enough.

Shipping Out

The depot was made up of a group of small two-story buildings. It didn't look much like an army camp. The cooking was done in one building while the feeding was done in the streets. There were always long chow lines and never enough seating. However, since there wasn't much to do at the depot, we were never in much of a hurry. Fortunately, the weather usually was good.

In the morning after chow we had an hour of calisthenics and then we went back to our bunks to write letters or play cards.

We were allowed passes to a small town within walking distance of the depot but we always had a 10 PM curfew. Unfortunately, there was little to do in town. An old mansion had been converted into an USO. It was run by middle-aged women but enough younger ladies were there to keep the soldiers interested in attending. Mostly we danced and drank a lot of tea.

Two young sisters lived near the camp. One of them was married and had children. Her husband was in the service. The other worked on a farm. In peacetime neither would never have gotten much attention. To the sex-starved Americans, however, they were beautiful. Equally important, they were *willing*. There were quite a few satisfied GIs.

After a few days we were shipped to a replacement depot to await our assignments. We didn't have much to do there, either, except write letters and think of our loved ones. Our mail had not caught up to us so the only comfort we had was to re-read the letters that we had received before we left. We were also short of money because our payroll records were not current.

Another soldier and I volunteered for night latrine duty. We did this not because we enjoyed cleaning toilets but in order to start a laundry business, since the latrine was equipped with a potbelly stove. We used this to heat our wash water and our flat iron. Our customer base was an outfit newly arrived in camp from fighting in Africa, who had brought with them duffle bags full of dirty clothes. Business was so brisk that in order to keep up with demand we would only scrub the collars of the shirts and press nice creases in the pants. They *looked* clean enough to pass inspection, which was what mattered.

To return the laundry, we hung the pants and

Shipping Out

shirts from a long pole, which my buddy and I would carry between us. The problem was that my partner was 6'4" and I was 5'8" so all the clothes shifted down to my end, forcing me to carry most of the weight. We were making a lot of extra money, though, and things were going well until we got orders to move on.

I was shipped out to join an Ordinance company formed mostly of men who had worked together at John Deere. The company was very cliquish and did not make newcomers feel welcome. We were billeted in the city of Warminster, in the center of town, in an old hotel that had been converted into a barracks. There were three-tier bunks and not much else. This was to be my home for almost a year.

Warminster

The city of Warminster consisted of eight streets. The food stores didn't have much to sell and were open for just a few hours in the morning. Everything was rationed. Even the stores that sold other types of merchandise had little to offer. In the center of town there was a movie house that showed British films, which were not too popular with the GIs, and some old American movies. We made the best of it.

American GIs took over two of the three pubs in town. The Americans would sit around and brag about how wonderful the U.S. was. This wasn't the right thing to do since the English had it tough because of the war. But they were polite and chalked up our rudeness to the fact that we were lonely.

From The Bronx to Berchtesgaden

Warminster, England, in the 1940s. Period postcard.

The depot where we were stationed was located past the outskirts of town. I was put to work repairing range finders, binoculars, and other fine instruments. These instruments were so delicate, the room had to be air-conditioned and dust proof. We had to work ten hours a day, six days a week. I bought a bicycle and on Sundays, after writing my letters home, I would go sightseeing. I visited Sherwood Forest, looking for the imaginary figure of Robin Hood, and saw castles by the dozen.

At the pub in town we met a gentlemen by the name of David Jones, who was in his early forties. He worked for the ministry in a nearby village. He invited a few of us to his home for conversation and tea and crumpets. We met his wife, Lucy, and his two

Warminster

children, a boy of ten and a girl of six. This was a typical English household. The outside gardens were well kept. Inside, everything was worn but comfortable. Houses were constructed of brick and stone.

It felt good sitting around the fireplace, having a bit of tea, and telling stories. We would bring over candy for the children from the PX and other items that were scarce to the English. We enjoyed hearing their slang expressions, such as, "Can I knock you up in the morning," which meant *wake you up*. They, in turn, made fun of our English. They called it *American*.

Just outside town was a meeting hall. On Saturday night they had an English version of our American Red Cross. Women served tea and crumpets and there was a band consisting of three older men and two women, who tried to play American music while the GIs tried to teach the English girls how to do the Lindy Hop. British soldiers on leave also attended the dance. They would gather on one side of the hall and chant, "The trouble with you Yanks is that you are over paid, over sexed, and over here."

There were apparently one hundred eligible women in town. Of these, 90 percent had GI boy-

From The Bronx to Berchtesgaden

friends, even though some of them were married. We had a young fellow in the company called Bob. He was not the going-out type but one day he came into the barracks in an excited state. He had a date with a Scottish girl who worked in a factory nearby. He described her as having long blonde hair and a nice figure. The next night he got dressed up and went to meet his date but he was back after only a short time. His date had caught her hair in a machine and it had been pulled from her scalp. He made arrangements to go to Scotland to visit her in the hospital. A few guys gave up part of their rations and sent him off with a big package of goodies for her.

One of our fellows was going with a married woman. Her English husband came home on leave. The lady spent the first week with her husband and then went back to seeing the GI. Still another of our boys decided to visit London with his English girlfriend. Unfortunately, he was broke because payroll was delayed. The young lady took two hundred dollars out of the family savings account and made him promise to pay it back before her husband came home. We were shipped out before our payroll caught up with us. But when

Warminster

it did, he sent her the money from France.

When most of the work was completed, we were ready for the invasion. Headquarters closed the depot and I was made a temporary MP working the night shift. There was an alleyway behind a group of houses, where the GIs would come out after having spent the night with their lady friends. Somehow I never caught anyone breaking curfew, nor did I want to. I was coming off duty one morning about 6 o'clock, when the sky turned black with hundreds of planes. I said to myself, *wouldn't it be nice if this were a prelude to the invasion?* When I awoke the next morning, the newscaster reported that the invasion was taking place.

After the initial assault, the allies needed reinforcements because of the tremendous losses of men and equipment on the beach. Luckily, there were some tanks at the depot, which had been repaired. It became our job to ferry them across the Channel. We were in landing craft in rough waters. The scene was devastating as we approached the beaches. There were bodies floating in the surf and many dead and dying on the sand. We turned over the tanks to another outfit and immediately headed back to England. I was seasick all the way and kept throwing up from both the rough water and from memories of the scene on the beach.

Shortly after we got back, we started our infantry training, which consisted of intense hiking and exercising. Then we started rifle practice, where they put a target two hundred yards away. I purposely missed the target by one hundred yards. When they moved the targets fifty yards closer, I still missed by fifty yards. The drill sergeant said, "I guess you can always use your bayonet," and passed me off as a rifleman.

After training, we were landed on the beaches of southern France. The 3rd Infantry Division had already cleared the beaches and that was where I came to join them.

Invasion

As we steamed towards the French coast, we could see the ships accompanying our vessel. There were gunships, other transport ships, cargo ships, even a battleship. The sky overhead was full of planes. We knew the time for jokes, false bravado, and loud talk had passed. It was time for prayer. I felt that I was completely alone and I kept thinking of things I should have said and done before I left home. But I was soon brought back to reality when I heard bombing off in the distance.

Before we loaded onto the landing craft, we were given new M1 rifles, combat clothing, and combat boots. These items lasted me for eight hundred miles, the distance I walked in Europe. We

From The Bronx to Berchtesgaden

American troops marching through a British port town on their way to the docks. Photo: Department of Defense.

were also loaded down with two bandoliers of ammunition, a bayonet, a first-aid packet, all of our own personal items, a raincoat, a blanket, two days' worth of rations, and a D bar. The D bar contained sugar, chocolate, skim milk powder, cocoa fat, and vanilla. This ration alone was able to sustain a man for a short period.

When I entered the Army, I weighed 175 pounds. Including all this equipment, I must have weighed at least 250 pounds. Then we climbed aboard the LSTs and we were on our way.

These transports were designed to deliver

Invasion

troops, tanks, and supplies right to the beach. The water was rough and we were all having a pretty bad time. Our ship kept hugging the coast to avoid German aircraft. Then, along with fifteen other boats, we headed toward shore in a straight formation.

As we neared the beach, we could hear the firing of shells in the distance. This was the real thing. We were entering the battle zone. One of the soldiers, a hillbilly from Tennessee, started to sing, interrupting my thoughts of home. I still remember the song he sang. "Send me a letter, send it by mail, and send it to the Birmingham jail."

My thoughts did not stray for long, seeing bodies floating in the water and many others on the beach. The sand was littered with burned-out tanks.

Approximately one hundred and twenty men of my group were joining the 7th Regiment of the 3rd Infantry Division as replacement riflemen.

As we disembarked, we were taken to the headquarters of the 7th Infantry Regiment to hear a briefing about the "Glorious Seventh." We were informed that the 7th Infantry was the oldest regiment in the U.S. Army, going back to the days of Andrew Jackson. They were also known as the

From The Bronx to Berchtesgaden

"Cotton Bailers", having gained the nickname because of the use they made of cotton bales in the battle for New Orleans during the War of 1812.

A colonel came to speak to us. "You are going up as replacements to the best damn regiment and division in this man's army," he said. "You will be expected to live up to that tradition. You will suffer and you will take it like men. You will learn to do your very best. Everyone is scared in his first battle. If he says he is not, he is a liar. The real hero is the one who fights even though he is scared."

In all the time I spent in battle, I never saw a colonel close to the front line of combat. Even so they wrote themselves up for many medals. They really could give the best damn speeches, though.

There were three men from the replacement depot still in my company. One of them was Jim Smith, who always thought everything was a joke. The war was a joke, in his opinion, but once he heard his first barrage, he changed his opinion fast. Most of the men sat and prayed. Then the group was broken up to join different companies. As we marched off, the sky was lit up with the continual flashing of an artillery barrage. We passed a stream of men

Invasion

An LST beached in France. Photo: U.S. Navy.

returning from the front and heading to the reserve. They were filthy, unshaven, and most had a vacant look in their eyes. Their comment to us was:

"It's hell up there."

The division was given a day off to reassemble so we had a chance to meet some of the veterans. Anyone who made it past their first encounter with the enemy was considered a veteran. They were a haggard bunch. The younger ones looked like school boys. Their jackets and trousers were filled with mud, which made us, the replacements, stand out in our clean uniforms. They were not anxious

From The Bronx to Berchtesgaden

to mingle with us. After I had some combat experience, I understood why the veterans were not anxious to make friends with the newcomers. I felt a little conspicuous in my new clean gear until I had a bit of mud splashed on it. I took out my clean shovel and I started to dig my first foxhole.

The following evening we had our baptism under fire. When the attack started, we were a group of inexperienced and scared men. Fortunately for me, I was in a reserve platoon. We had not gone more than one hundred yards when our point platoon man stepped into an area of Schu mines, nicknamed Bouncing Betties. These mines were designed to wound soldiers instead of killing them. They were planted beneath the ground in metal containers that held hundreds of steel balls. When stepped upon, they exploded and flew into the air at waist height. We could hear the agonizing screams of wounded men and their calls for medics. There was nothing anyone could do to help them. The wounded soldiers were markers for the rest of us. They showed the rest of the company where the mines were so we could skirt the minefield and go on.

One of the fellows with me right from the be-

Invasion

ginning at the induction center was Bob Silver. He was even more frightened and homesick than most. He clung to me like a shadow. Bob did his best to get into the same company I was in. Unfortunately, he was put in the unlucky platoon on his first night in combat. His platoon was the one that was caught in the minefield, and Bob was killed.

It was dark so we stayed close to the man in front of us. As I jumped into a ditch, there was a GI lying in the hole. Thinking he was stalling, I pushed him to move. He turned over and I saw he was dead. Then I took off and kept running until I was ahead of the company. When I was transferred from Ordinance to the Infantry, I thought to myself that since there were 180 men in the company, I would be the 179th. Here I found myself at the head of the company. The Germans all seemed to be shooting at me, and the next shell could blow me to hell. I panicked, wanting to run back, but it was dark and I didn't know which way to run so I stayed where I was and prayed.

A few hundred yards ahead we were stopped by enemy resistance. This consisted of scattered strong points supported by artillery fire. The barrage of German shells was constant. They launched with

From The Bronx to Berchtesgaden

a regular hammering rhythm. The ground trembled on impact. The vibrations were frightening. This sensation, however, was also reassuring because it meant the shells had missed you.

There was nothing we could do but lie there and take it. One shell in particular seemed to have my number on it. Its whine was high pitched and continued longer than any I had heard before. I thought it was coming for me. I prayed furiously and kept my body as flat as possible. When the shell finally hit, my entire body bounced up into the air as my breath was knocked out of me. Thank God I was otherwise unhurt.

That evening when I opened my pack, I discovered that my blanket was full of holes. The shrapnel from the near miss had passed completely through my pack. The shell had my number on it, sure enough, but its calibration had been off by a hair. It wasn't my time to go. Even though the ground was hard, I continued to dig furiously with my shovel, pounding away to make sure the hole was sufficiently deep to protect me.

The shelling continued for three hours. It felt like an eternity. All you could do was lie there and

Invasion

anticipate the moment that would end your life. No amount of training could really prepare a man for combat. Training got a person physically fit and prepared to use a weapon, but it did not prepare you to lie helplessly under a barrage of artillery bombardment and machine-gun fire for hours on end, listening to the indescribable sounds of war. But after your first battle, if you still lived, you had proven yourself. You had a good idea of what to expect and what was expected of you. You and your fellow soldiers were no longer strangers thrown together randomly by war but hardened veterans of battle.

Peering over the lip of my foxhole, I saw a movement in the bushes. I sighted down the barrel of my M1 rifle and squeezed the trigger and the German soldier became still and I realized that I had killed a man.

I told myself that he was a German and that Germans were the enemy. I knew that if I hadn't shot him first, he would have killed me, and I knew that I would do the same again when I had to. He was the first man I ever killed but he was not to be the last.

My platoon leader, a first lieutenant, approached me and said they were short of noncoms. He'd noticed that I had handled myself well and thought that I had leadership ability so he was going to put in a request to promote me to sergeant. Soon I was in charge of a twelve-man squad. I could not figure out whether to be happy or frightened about taking on this responsibility.

Sergeant Soskil

I tried not to get too friendly with the men in my squad. After our first battle as a team, however, we bonded tightly because of the experiences we had shared. We were all changing from young civilians into killers aged beyond our years.

At the end of the first day's fighting, less than half of our platoon was left. Most of the casualties were lying behind us in mine fields or on the approaches to the German positions that we had succeeded in overrunning.

A wounded German soldier lay one hundred and fifty yards away from me. A German medic ran onto the field. In addition to a red cross on his helmet he had a white apron with a red cross on it tied around his body. Our boys did not fire

From The Bronx to Berchtesgaden

on him. Instead of treating the wounded German soldier, however, the medic reached into his bag, drew out a grenade, and threw it at us. The boys quickly made an end of that liar but three of our men were hit and they were in agony.

Nothing tore at your insides more than hearing a wounded man cry out in pain for help when there was nothing you could do for him. We had run out of morphine and bandages.

In the early hours of darkness the platoon sergeant and I reorganized our remaining men. We obtained some ammunition, ate some C rations, and awaited further instructions from the company commander. Around midnight, orders came to press the attack. We led the assault until 0300, when we entered an area known as the Dickerwald.

At daylight the Germans counterattacked with a Mark VI tank supported by twenty-five infantry. We had run out of bazooka ammunition but we drove off the German soldiers with rifle fire, killing most of them. The tank pulled back and fired from a distance.

They had us pinned down, unable to move from our foxholes. A shell landed near where I was crouching. My head was spinning and I felt disoriented.

Sergeant Soskil

Then my platoon corporal, a man named Bergmann, jumped in beside me and let out a wise crack.

"Is this your way of spending a nice day at home?" he asked.

"I earned my pay my first day in combat," I answered, not at all amused.

The sun came out. We looked up into the sky and saw a group of our fighter planes. We heard the explosion of their bombs and the rattle of their machine guns. Their attack gave us the freedom to escape from our foxholes—*hell pits*, we called them. I gathered my squad together to move forward. One of our soldiers refused to join us. He was soaked in blood from the corpse sharing his foxhole.

Just a short while previously this corpse had been a human being with hopes for the future. The dead soldier was someone's brother, son, or friend. His suffering was over but those who loved him would go on suffering and hurting forever. In his pockets we found pictures of his family and one of a pretty young lady who might have been his sweetheart.

After a tough fight, we advanced and captured a fort manned by Italians and Vichy French backed by SS troopers. It required some time to

From The Bronx to Berchtesgaden

break their resistance and we took many prisoners. On entering town, we captured a three-man mortar crew. The Germans did not act like supermen. They were scared. They took family pictures from their pockets and held them out for sympathy. Then a German officer with his men came in to surrender. They brought with them leaflets promising safe conduct if they surrendered peacefully. We honored this promise.

As much as I would have liked to revenge myself upon the Germans, it was more important that we bring them back for questioning. The GIs kept waving their guns at the Germans and threatening

French North African soldiers. Photo: Department of Defense.

Sergeant Soskil

them but held off. When you were killing and being killed, something happened to the mind. The opposing soldier became less human. These were the same guys who had been shooting at you and may have killed your buddies.

Pushing on to the city of Orange, we were joined by a battalion of French Moroccans. Some of them traveled with their mules and wives, in that order. If there was shelter, they would put the mules in first. Then, if there were any room left, the wives would be permitted to take cover. Their battalion included a section of ten tanks. When we were stopped by a German strong point, their tanks formed a circle around the strong point. Like American Indians attacking covered wagons, the Moroccan tanks would fire at the strong point, run, and then return for another shot. They knocked out their objective but lost four tanks. At night, even though the enemy was close by, they lit huge bonfires to cook their meals. That, of course, drew enemy fire. We were happy to see the Moroccans leave to rejoin a French outfit.

Our next big encounter found us at the approach to the Vosges Mountains, which had never been crossed

From The Bronx to Berchtesgaden

by a military force opposed by an enemy. As the Germans fell back, their withdrawals became shorter and their resistance became stronger. At the Moselle River, the enemy dug in, using mines, booby traps, and roadblocks to stop our advance.

The Germans were tricky in setting booby traps. Our GIs were notorious souvenir hunters. The enemy would wire their dead and even their wounded ... a door, a window ... just about anything. Most infantrymen would not keep any German equipment for fear that if they were captured, they would be treated badly or shot. The Germans would think they were the ones responsible for the death of their comrades.

We had some heavy fighting and lost a quarter of our company but eventually we broke through. Then we were sent to the regiment reserve to refill our company with replacements and to get some rest.

The replacements kept getting younger. They were coming from all parts of the country as the need for men became urgent. Most of them had just turned eighteen. Fellows that were green soldiers today were veterans tomorrow. Unfortunately, the replacements didn't have much training and they were

Sergeant Soskil

3rd Algerian Division. Photo: Department of Defense.

thrown into battle unprepared for what they would face. Many became casualties the first day. On the other hand, it was rare that any officer above the rank of captain was ever seen when there was combat.

It was nighttime as I led my squad a few blocks from the center of the town of Villeninfroy. We were receiving small arms fire from snipers. We passed a burning building that lit up the area. There wasn't much cover as each house had an iron picket fence. To advance we would have to go out in the street or over the fences in order not to expose ourselves. All the doors were securely locked. I blasted

From The Bronx to Berchtesgaden

the locks off one door and half the squad went into the house and the other half started going over the backyard fences. When we came to the last house, we were at the town square, where we were joined by the rest of the company.

Under town hall we discovered a community wine vat the size of a large room. Some GIs decided to go swimming in the wine vat. After swallowing some wine and breathing in the fumes, we had a happy bunch of soldiers. For us it was a funny scene but the townspeople were not happy. Fortunately, we had a few days of relief because many of the GIs were seeing double. After a good shower and some rest, however, they were once again ready for combat.

When our supplies came up, we each received three boxes of K-rations and a canteen of water. If more were needed, we would have to melt snow to replenish our canteens. More important to me was to get enough ammunition for my weapons. I carried a M1 Tommy gun and a .45 pistol, which used the same caliber ammunition as the machine gun. To round things out, I had four grenades hung on my jacket.

Sergeant Soskil

The fun was soon over and once again we started to advance. Enemy resistance kept getting stronger. They were so dug in, we had to use bayonets and grenades to dig them out. We kept pushing on until we took the town of Lune. Afterwards, we repulsed a counterattack by a tank and an assault by some two hundred frenzied Germans. Many of them were shouting in English that they wanted to die for Hitler. They rushed into our fire insanely, as if they had been given drugs before the assault. We did our best to accommodate their death wish.

During the fighting, one of my soldiers was hit. A medic, carrying a flag with the red cross on it, went out to attend him. The medic was targeted by a German sniper and killed. So I crawled out thirty yards and dragged the wounded soldier back to our command post myself. After the war I found out that this wounded soldier had lived and made it home. For this deed I was awarded the Bronze Star, the fourth-highest combat award of the U.S. Armed Forces.

We were now only a short distance from the headwaters of the Moselle River. We were in our foxholes for the night, when my corporal called out:

From The Bronx to Berchtesgaden

"Do you want to see a bunch of Germans?"

I turned my head and saw a whole group of them coming at us from across a snow-covered mountain. They were wearing white coverings over their uniforms. It seemed like there were hundreds of the enemy even though there were only dozens. Then their shelling started. I lay face down as the shells hit all around me, throwing up snow and steel fragments, and I told myself that I should have dug a deeper foxhole. When the shelling stopped, we heard the rumbling of tanks. They emerged from the woods behind the infantry. As they advanced, they reversed positions and the infantry got behind the tanks as our rifle fire slowed them down.

Our own artillery opened up with anti-tank guns. They disabled two of the tanks and set them on fire. The screams of the soldiers in the tanks made us shudder but the remaining 88s kept firing. One of the shells hit the branches of the tree above me and a branch struck me on the helmet. Many men around me were dead. The remaining German tanks withdrew and the battle was over.

As usual, after much hard fighting and as we neared our objective, politics came into play. After

Sergeant Soskil

we took the town, a French unit relieved us and we had to give them the credit for the victory.

As we moved towards the Belfast Gap, we had to wade through waist-deep streams, hike through heavily-wooded mountains, and be ready to attack in early morning. We met some intense opposition but beat off nine counterattacks by fanatical Nazis, who yelled allegiance to Hitler as they attacked. We held our position but lost quite a few men.

We were told by a prisoner that the Germans used screaming and yelling in their charges as a scare tactic. This startled some of our new replacements but not our hardened combat veterans.

We moved so fast that the Germans abandoned hundreds of trucks and field pieces as they fled across the bridge over the Moselle. The bridge had been prepared for demolition but we gave them no time to destroy it. Then once again, after fighting, we were relieved by the French. As I said, there are politics even in war.

That night I got a severe toothache. After some looking, I finally located a dentist. My cheek was swollen and the tooth had abscessed. It had to come out. Unfortunately, the dentist did not have any pain medication or proper medical tools. He had to extract my tooth with a pair of pliers and without anesthetic. I had a fever for two days but, minus one tooth, still stayed with my outfit.

Our next objective was Bemont, which was secured after heavy fighting and a repulsed counterattack. We continued without much resistance until we crossed the Meurthe River on a footbridge. At this point we encountered the enemy's winter line, which consisted of zigzag fire trenches, machine gun emplacements, and concrete bunkers. One bunker in particular had us stopped for two hours and we couldn't move.

Silver Star

A barrage of artillery, mortar, and machine-gun fire pinned us down. The noise from the German shells was constant. For two hours, an eternity, shells were launched at us with a regular hammering rhythm. As night fell, I wired back for smoke to give us cover. It was a long, agonizing wait, but finally the battalion responded with smoke. A wounded man in my platoon was carrying a dynamite satchel. I took this from him and I crawled on my hands and knees into a low trench, which ran almost to the bunker. With a quick rush, I reached the side of the pillbox. I deposited the dynamite satchel through the opening and ran for cover. The blast killed all the German soldiers inside and I got shook up with a splitting headache from the noise.

From The Bronx to Berchtesgaden

Interior of a German underground dugout complete with a brass bed. Photo: Imperial War Museum.

For exemplary heroism I was awarded the Silver Star, which is the third-highest combat military decoration that can be awarded to a soldier.

The bunker was three stories deep. On the bottom level there were pictures on the walls, furniture, running water, toilet facilities, and stacks of canned goods, all the comforts of home. On the bottom floor eight women were still alive. Four of them were in German uniforms and the others wore civilian clothes. One of our GIs picked out a pretty girl and said he was going to take care of her. He took her to a nearby farmhouse, where they could be alone.

Silver Star

He meant to have sex with her but she got hold of a pair of scissors and castrated him instead. When we heard his screams coming from the farmhouse, the rest of us ran to see what had happened. The GI had bled to death. The German woman was also dead.

Our orders were to knock out the remaining bunkers. There were less than a dozen men left alive in my squad. To our surprise and relief we found the next bunker unoccupied, but the rest of them were fully manned. Since I felt that my platoon had already done its fair share of fighting that day, I instructed the men to return to the first bunker to get some rest for the remainder of the night. When we ventured out in the morning, we were surrounded—by

A German bunker. Photo: Bernard Chenal.

From The Bronx to Berchtesgaden

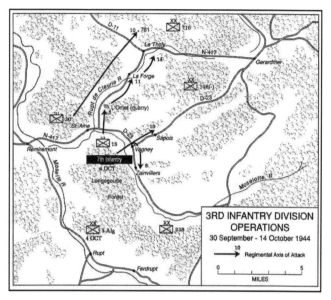

Source: United States Army in World War II, European Theater of Operations, Riviera to the Rhine.

friendly troops. General Patton had broken through and the enemy had abandoned their defensive line.

The next phase of this push was a sweep into the Alsatian Plains, cleaning scores of enemy from the towns on the way. There was a pocket of one hundred Germans who wanted to continue fighting but after receiving heavy casualties, they surrendered. I was watching one SS trooper, a strong blond Aryan who seemed ten feet tall. As he bent down, I saw him take something shiny out of his boot. My instinct and

Silver Star

experience told me not to hesitate. I raised my rifle and fired. I was right. He was holding something in his hand. I discovered that the shiny object was a .22 caliber pistol with a chrome body and a pearl handle. Thankful for having one less enemy to worry about, I took the pistol for myself and I still have it today.

As we approached the Muertha River, we heard explosions in the distance. The Germans were methodically destroying the city of Saint-Dié-des-Vosges.

Over the city was a big cloud of smoke. Around us were the burned dead bodies of humans and beasts. As we approached St. Dié, we saw that the city was on fire. The Germans had killed everyone they could find and torched the place.

For awhile we did not see a living soul. Suddenly an old woman stepped out of the rubble and asked us:

"Americans?"

When we said *yes*, she turned to the rubble and yelled, "Americans!"

Soon people started to appear. They were all shaken up and crying. We did our best to calm them down. We handed out cigarettes and some of our rations. We tried to convince them that help

From The Bronx to Berchtesgaden

was on the way. The townspeople told us stories of German atrocities. Local men had been castrated in public and the Germans had dragged the bodies of American POWs through the streets behind cars. These stories would have been hard for us to believe had it not been for the passion in their voices and the tears in the eyes of the townspeople as they told us the tales. As we left town, the French civilians lined both side of the streets and sang their national anthem to us.

Next we came to the Colmar Pocket, the flat

An American mortar crew. Photo: US Office of War Information.

Silver Star

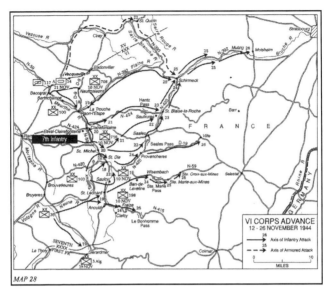

Source: United States Army in World War II, European Theater of Operations, Riviera to the Rhine.

plains south of Strasbourg between the Vosges Mountains and the Rhine River. Here the French First Army joined us, although they were of little help and the 3rd Infantry Division still had to do most of the fighting. The high temperature during the day was ten degrees Fahrenheit and at night it fell below zero. On the ground were several feet of snow. The area was dotted with stone houses, each of which was a potential fort, and the Germans made a serious effort to defend the area.

In preparation for the attack all our vehicles

From The Bronx to Berchtesgaden

were painted white, and white gowns were given to the foot solders. Bridging materials were being assembled for another river crossing. Here the French forces left us. A massive artillery barrage preceded our advance to compensate for our lack of armor. Unfortunately, the bright shining moon took away any concealment, and clearly illuminated us as we struggled, heavily-laden, through the snow.

Suddenly two German tanks appeared before us. German infantry followed the tanks with rifle and machine-gun fire. We were trapped in the open field without cover. Many of our men were killed and the rest hit the ground and started to dig with their hands. Once our artillery started to return the fire, however, we were able to take a breather. The remnants of the battalion rushed for the village ahead. When I got there, my heart was pounding and my lungs were burning. I came to a stone wall and climbed over it, dragging my equipment behind me, and joined some other soldiers from my platoon.

We took cover behind one of the buildings and waited for orders to move out. When they came, I edged out with two members of my squad, so we might see where the gunfire was coming from. These

Silver Star

French civilians search through the rubble of their town.
Photo: National Archives.

two men were on either side of me. A German machine gun opened up and both soldiers were hit but the bullets missed me completely. By this miracle I knew my family back home was looking after me.

Our troops reorganized and we got the bazooka team together. We gathered up all the ammunition we could find and started to fire at the tanks even though they were out of range. This used up most of our ammo. Finally, as the tanks came within range, the bazooka team hit one with their last rocket, setting it on fire.

One of our soldiers attempted to knock out another tank with a rifle grenade. In his excitement he

From The Bronx to Berchtesgaden

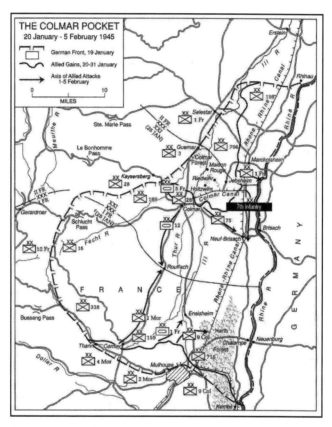

Source: United States Army in World War II, European Theater of Operations, Riviera to the Rhine.

used a live bullet instead of a blank to launch the grenade. The grenade exploded in his face, causing him serious injury. After this incident the men had a little more confidence in the bazooka.

Fighting became heavy again as we approached

Silver Star

the suburbs of Strasbourg. We were pinned down by machine gun and mortar fire. Some of the new replacements refused to leave their foxholes even though the mortar barrage was getting closer. As squad leader, it was my job to motivate them. This required much threatening and yelling but finally I got them moving. Just before the center of town was a group of houses, which an enemy machine-gun crew was using as a strong point. We rushed the houses, throwing hand grenades through windows, killing the machine-gun crew and capturing a few more prisoners, who seemed happy to surrender. These prisoners were not die-hard SS troopers. They were Romanian and Hungarian soldiers conscripted into the German army.

At the outskirts of town a soldier next to me was hit by a sniper. The bullet sliced across his stomach, spilling his intestines on the ground. I yelled for the medics and tried to gather his insides together. He lived for awhile but died later. The sniper who shot him was hidden in a church but we found him and killed him to avenge our companion.

Unfortunately, the Germans were established in deep dugouts and bunkers. Our attack pro-

From The Bronx to Berchtesgaden

gressed to within two hundred yards of our objective, where it was halted due to great numbers of casualties. Many men ran out of ammunition and started to fix bayonets to their rifles. We were about to attack with what weapons we had, when our supply trucks arrived with ammunition, enabling us to contain the Germans. The enemy finally retreated. They had also suffered heavy losses.

The artillery barrage kept up all night as we fought desperately for the town. The same buildings changed hands several times in several hours. Houses burned and walls crumbled, blown apart by shells and wrecked by grenades. We used bazookas to make holes in the walls to get from house to house under cover. Then I would throw in a grenade and charge through with a blast of bullets from my Tommy gun.

Moving forward again, we came to the Rhine Marne Canal. We were caught in an open field under heavy shelling. We were to charge across a wooded area held by the Germans. Everyone was running and yelling. This was like something from a movie. The frenzy gave our men courage but the enemy was frightened and dispirited. Many German soldiers tried to surrender but our boys were

Silver Star

so riled up, they didn't give them a chance to do so. All our GIs wanted to do at that point was to kill Germans. They were mad with battle lust.

Our tanks sprayed the paths with machine-gun fire and with their 75s. The tanks made holes in the houses for the infantry to enter. We battled from floor to floor and room to room. After we had taken a few hundred prisoners, and things quieted down, my hands started to shake. During battle I had no time to think or to be afraid but afterward my fear and fright caught up with me. Even so I prayed that I would never forget to be afraid, that I would not get careless, that I would stay alive.

Across the Moselle

A shell landed near our lieutenant, throwing him up in the air and knocking him unconscious. Otherwise, however, he was unscratched. He was taken by medics to the rear but soon came back to rejoin our company.

Our artillery did a good job of quieting the Germans down and after a little resistance the entire battalion reached the canal. It was fifty feet wide. The engineers tied together two barges to make a bridge and we walked over it in single file to the other bank. We continued on the other side for a quarter of a mile until we came to the banks of the Moselle River.

When dawn arrived, and it started to get light, the enemy began shelling us with 88s and 105s.

From The Bronx to Berchtesgaden

The shells were dropping all around us. Some men panicked and tried to swim the canal to get back to the other side. The canal was deep and some of the men couldn't swim and they drowned but most got across. After taking a pounding for several days, we ran short of rations and water. We were getting desperate until the supply wagon arrived.

Once again we started over the two barges and approached the other side of the canal. Then the engineers came with assault boats. There were two engineers and twelve infantrymen in each boat. Our artillery barrage pulverized the Germans, killing many, and most fled.

Crossing the Moselle. Photo Department of Defense.

Across the Moselle

GIs read the 3rd Infantry Division paper, *The Front Line*. Photo: U.S. Army.

The river was swollen by autumn rains and was too swift and deep to be crossed by foot troops. Rather than risk a frontal attack, we were commanded to construct footbridges and use the darkness of night to surprise the enemy. We drew a damp moonless night for the crossing. Fortunately, we met little resistance since other American troops were crossing in different places, drawing away enemy troops from our area.

Throughout the following day we battled German infantry. We also encountered Schu mines, trip-wire booby traps, and machine-gun fire. There were still enough enemy soldiers left behind to give us trouble. For two days we were practically without food and water. The mines made movement of supplies and the evacuation of the wounded difficult. The engineers finally cleared a path so that supplies started coming through. Most important to me was that the mail arrived. I received six letters from Pearl and a stack of envelopes from the family. I couldn't wait until daylight to start reading.

Writing and receiving mail was what kept us going and kept us sane. I kept reading the letters over and over again until I had them memorized. Some of the fellows did not receive mail. We shared some of the news from our wives and girlfriends with them. A joke or funny story was always read aloud but still there were many tears of loneliness.

One of the soldiers received a newspaper from home. In disbelief we learned that the Army was shipping German POWs back to the States. They were being given good sleeping quarters, plenty of food, and hot coffee with their meals. Many had jobs working in military posts or harvesting crops and were actually being paid ninety cents an hour for their labor. German POWs

Across the Moselle

could buy goods in our PXs and many were allowed into town for recreation.

Our boys were not thrilled by this news. We knew the Germans treated their own prisoners of war like animals. But mail from the front was censored and the people back home, even the media, had little idea of the atrocities the Germans were inflicting on American POWs.

I received packages from my folks and my sisters. They had given up some of their ration points to send me salamis. Unfortunately, these had gotten rock-hard in transit. Pearl had baked cookies and rolled them in cellophane. They were quickly devoured. She also sent orange marmalade, which we happened to have plenty of already. It was the thought that counted, however, and tears came to my eyes. I knew my wife and family were hoping and praying for my safe return.

It was one battle after another, day in and day out. Many of my buddies were wounded or dead. I kept waiting for my turn to come. I was so depressed, I couldn't trust myself to speak. I kept thinking, "Why me? Why me?"

Near the edge of town we encountered a group

From The Bronx to Berchtesgaden

of forts, which had been part of the French Maginot Line. This was supposed to be the French line of defense before the Nazis invaded but it hadn't given the Germans much trouble. The Germans simply went around the Line when they invaded the country. These forts were built below ground and were surrounded by moats twenty feet wide. It took quite an effort by our army engineers to ren-

Bunkers of the French Maginot Line. Photo: National Archives.

Across the Moselle

Nazi propaganda poster.

der them useless with plenty of dynamite.

We moved into the bunkers but the Germans returned with new 88s and tanks and drove us out.

From The Bronx to Berchtesgaden

Then we counterattacked with artillery fire that caused the enemy heavy casualties. At times the battle raged inside the bunkers. There was hand-to-hand fighting with knives and pistols. Both sides took casualties and finally we were ordered to fall back to a new position along the Moder River. Here we remained for a week under the worst conditions imaginable. We suffered from the weather and from shortages of food and water. We were even out of clean socks, which were necessary to prevent our feet from rotting.

After some fighting, the division captured Strasbourg, a beautiful and ancient city, which was a hotbed of German influence and French collaborators. Some Nazi and SS diehards tried to make a stand but the Infantry alone made short work of them. We quickly moved in. After witnessing so much of the ruin of war, it was surprising to see lovely homes and tree-lined streets. When the Army made a strategic withdrawal, the French people, fearing the Germans' return, quickly removed all the U.S. and French flags from their windows and replaced them with swastikas, which they had taken down previously. As we were leaving the city, they spat at us from windows above the street.

Across the Moselle

I saw a poster in a store window with a cartoon drawing of Uncle Sam. He had a hefty sack of dollars clutched in his hand and a dog collar around his neck. A hunchbacked, unshaven Jew, who had a hooked nose and wore a rich man's coat, was leading Uncle Sam on a leash. Being a Jewish American soldier, I couldn't contain myself so I took my carbine and smashed the window and tore down the poster.

Our next move was to cross the Ill River. We captured a bridge but as our first tank started across, the span collapsed, leaving us without tank support. It was during this battle that Audie Murphy, who was the most decorated soldier in the Army, added the Medal of Honor to his other decorations. We were deep in the woods when the Germans counterattacked. Murphy ran out thirty yards to a burning tank destroyer and, manning its .50 caliber machine gun, turned back an assault of two hundred and fifty Germans and three tanks, killing thirty-five of the enemy. Although wounded and covered with soot, he held the enemy at bay. He then directed artillery fire at the advancing tanks. It was enough to make them retreat. He received the Medal of Honor and for our division work at the

From The Bronx to Berchtesgaden

The fortress town of Neuf-Brisach. Photo: Department of Defense.

Colmar Pocket, we received the Cross de Guerre. After the war, Audie Murphy made three movies in Hollywood. He died in a civilian airplane crash.

We went into division reserve and pulled back between the cities of Metz and Nancy after 168 days of constant contact with the enemy. I was allowed three days in rest camp. We were given new clothes and a chance to take real showers. After being in the same uniform for three months and having to use our helmets as washbasins, this was a real luxury. We even ate some hot meals. I almost felt human after six months in hell. We also received our back

Across the Moselle

mail. The letters brought me up to date with what was happening with my loved ones back home. Of course, I was happy to receive my letters, but it also brought a deep longing to be home with my family.

We were not allowed to divulge our whereabouts in our letters just in case the enemy captured our mail. In order to let my folks back home know where I was, in one of my letters I sent regards to our friend Roz's parents, whose name, coincidentally, was Metz. It was a bit of a secret message.

I learned that my sister's boyfriend was stationed in Metz so I went to visit him. I started out at daylight and I was able to get a hitch to his company. When I started back to my outfit, however, it was getting dark and nobody would give me a lift. I had to run the entire twelve miles on foot. It was a frightening journey, which took me through several burned-out towns. The corpses of dead animals littered the roadside. Gun fire boomed intermittently in the distance. I had a hard time seeing where I was going but I was grateful for the darkness because I was afraid of being targeted by Nazi snipers, who were infamous for their accuracy. When I finally reached camp just as the sun started to rise,

From The Bronx to Berchtesgaden

I was exhausted but glad to be alive.

Upon my return, I heard we would have to break camp. This upset me so much I was on the verge of going AWOL. It didn't seem fair that I had to return to battle so soon while the cadre officers in charge at rest camp would never see combat. They had a great deal. They had the French women to wash their clothes for them, to cook their meals, and to serve them in many other ways.

Our general told us that President Roosevelt and Prime Minister Churchill had held a summit conference at Yalta in the Crimea. Great decisions had been made to occupy Germany and liberate other countries after the fighting ceased. This information heartened the men. What we heard was that the war was almost over. We were weary of battle and ready to let someone else finish the job. Some men joked in a spirit of assumed selflessness that there was more than enough honor to go around, and it was only proper that our division members share the honor with other combat troops in the theater.

Unfortunately, however, much tough fighting still lay ahead of us.

Continuing our push forward, we went a few

Across the Moselle

miles and stopped for the night and once again dug our foxholes. Darkness came early since it was the middle of winter. With the night came penetrating cold.

We heard the squeaking and roaring of Panzers. I passed the word for everyone to stay in their holes and let the tanks roll over us. The tanks were moving and firing fast. We got down as far as possible in the icy water filling the bottoms of our holes.

The tanks rolled right over us without stopping and came within a few yards of the pillboxes. They fired armor-piercing shells against the pillboxes, turning them into smoldering piles of rubble. Then they turned and rumbled away, rolling over our foxholes again, thankfully without doing much damage and without noticing us huddling beneath them.

As we approached the walls of Neuf-Brisach, we encountered a railway bridge. Our scouting patrol found a demolition charge that had been laid by the Germans to destroy the bridge but it was still intact. The enemy never had a chance to blow it up. The patrol also reported enemy traffic evacuating from the other side of town. Our battalion officer ordered our artillery, our tanks, and mortar fire to be laid on this traffic. We annihilated the enemy.

From The Bronx to Berchtesgaden

Near the bridge we came across a civilian who, after some persuasion, agreed to assist us. He jumped down into the dry moat and led the platoon through a narrow passage through the walls into town. The town was built to withstand a siege, but fortunately our method of attack made a direct assault unnecessary.

There was little fighting and we captured one hundred prisoners. After this battle the 3rd Infantry was recognized by the War Department for outstanding performance of duty in action. We received the Presidential Unit Citation.

On March 13th combat regiments of the 3rd Infantry Division began moving under cover of darkness to assembly areas fifty miles north of Strasbourg and Nancy in northern Lorraine, just inside France on the former Franco-German border. It seemed as though the top brass had waited for me to get back from rest camp before striking a new offensive. I barely had time to pack my kit before the division started back into line. In the gray dawn we passed the dugouts and foxholes of the 44th Division troops.

I heard one fellow say, "We wish you men

Across the Moselle

luck, but honestly, we're sure as hell and very glad it's you and not us."

Someone in my squad answered, "Yeah, and buddy, thanks a lot. See you in hell."

The division move to the Franco-German border was secret. The numbers on vehicle bumpers were covered over. Shoulder patches were blotted out with strips of adhesive, as were the blue-and-white patches that decorated helmets.

Colonel Huntges, the commander of the 7th Regiment, and Colonel Duncan, commander of our battalion, ordered an attack. Unfortunately, their intelligence about the enemy's strength was incorrect. They had been told that we were only to receive token resistance. But we soon encountered Schu mines as well as anti-tank mines. We sustained serious causalities right from the start. Four tanks were disabled and the balance of our attached armor was halted. We used up most of our bazooka ammunition. Our communications were not in place and we were unable to keep in touch with our artillery. Even so we pushed into Utweiller, capturing the town and taking many prisoners. We were inside Germany.

Germany

Two hours after the siege ended, a battalion of enemy infantry, supported by nine tank destroyers and four Flakwagons, ringed the town on three sides. They methodically leveled any houses in their path. Without supporting armor, our only alternative to annihilation was withdrawal. I had my squad at the edge of town. As the officer in charge, I told my men that I would run first to the next house, they should count to ten, and the next man should run. The soldier that was supposed to run after me got nervous and ran ahead. As he passed between the two houses, an 88 hit him and he disappeared. I did not look back.

I ran a gauntlet of machine gun and rifle fire. My helmet was knocked off as I ran. In short rushes, I sped past a tank, which was still firing away. Nearing the last house, I encountered a machine-gun nest with six Germans in it. With a look of startled terror in his eyes, a German officer tried to raise his Luger. Fortunately, I was a little faster than he was. The five other Germans in the nest surrendered. Lining the prisoners up before me, I herded my prisoners back to headquarters.

The battalion had six hundred men when we started the attack. Fewer than fifty survived. The rest were killed, wounded, or captured. I helped find the division a new route forward while riding on a tank, skirting the enemy mine field. The division then formed a bazooka unit, supported by fifteen pieces of armor. We launched a counterattack behind an artillery preparation, retaking the town. In doing so we destroyed seven enemy tanks and four Flakwagons. For this I received another Silver Star for heroism.

I was called to battalion headquarters, where a colonel from regimental headquarters approached me. He said they were short of seasoned officers and that he had *carte blanche* to promote noncom officers with field commissions. He asked

Germany

me to accept a promotion. After a little thought, I declined. Even though I had gone through quite a bit as a dogface foot soldier, I didn't want to make a change. Besides, the average lifetime of an officer in our company was two weeks.

I thought the colonel would bust a gut when I turned down the promotion. Although I had just received the Silver Star for heroism, he called me a coward.

"Sir," I responded, "suppose I don't want to transfer, can you order me to?"

"You're a sergeant and I am a colonel. I sure

Crossing the Siegfried Line. Photo: National Archives.

From The Bronx to Berchtesgaden

can," he said.

"Well, sir," I replied, "after fighting across Europe, and considering that the end of the war is near, I would prefer staying with my company, sir."

I guess that was the reason I did not get any more promotions.

We took a few more towns and approached the fortification called the Siegfried Line. This structure consisted of three rows of four-feet-high concrete triangles, called *dragon's teeth*, separated by deep v-shaped ditches, which were meant to stop tanks. It also contained complexes of bunkers connected to each other by networks of trenches and tunnels.

Preparations were made to attack the Line. We were given extra ammunition and rations. Before the attack started, we looked up from our foxholes and saw hundreds of planes on a bombing run. They were English. Suddenly to our horror we saw that the planes were aiming their bombs on the ground where we were. Apparently a breeze had pushed the smoke line, which the bombers used for targeting, back from the enemy position and over our own location. As one man we all dove for our foxholes. Rattling down through the

Germany

The Siegfried Line. Photo: Department of Defense.

air fell swarms of bombs. There is no way to describe their sound and fury. Minutes seemed like hours as explosives rained down upon us.

Finally the bombing stopped, moved a mile away, and began falling over the German line. Unfortunately, the error had been caught too late. Some of our soldiers were suffering from shell shock and had to be sent back to the rear. It had been a horrific encounter. Our allies made a huge blunder. I was sure there were many tears shed by the bomber crews back in England.

Our night attack faced strong resistance. The

From The Bronx to Berchtesgaden

Germans met us with artillery, mortars, and machine-gun fire. Just before dawn they launched a counterattack that was so furious it almost succeeded in driving us back. But our side inflicted so many casualties upon the enemy in return that their resistance weakened.

Our battalion spent three hours on artillery preparation of the Line, which ripped at the bunkers and dragon's teeth. We started forward. Before the dragon's teeth were anti-tank ditches twelve feet wide. Then there were bunkers. I got as far as the dragon's teeth and there I was pinned down. I took cover below a ledge in front of the teeth. Suddenly a cluster of German mortar shells came screaming in. Every infantryman knew from experience that the higher the pitch at the beginning and the longer the scream, the closer the shells were coming. The shell that got me began at the top of the register and just kept coming and coming. I flattened my tummy and buttocks against the ground and braced myself for the shock. The shell hit five feet behind me. I felt myself bounce and I knew I had been hit.

Luckily, my wounds consisted only of some

Germany

pebbles or shrapnel in my backside. I had the battalion medics clean and bandage me, as I did not want to go to the hospital. I was fearful that they would send a "wounded in action" letter to my folks. Generally, this type of letter never stated how bad the wound really was. I knew that if my family received such a letter, they would take the news badly and assume that I had been gravely injured. Of course, not going to the hospital was a mistake. If I had, I would have received a Purple Heart. Ironically, some GIs were in the hospital with venereal disease. Even so, they received Purple Hearts, as one was thrown on every bed in the hospital, regardless of why the patient was there.

After this attack our three companies were reduced to the size of a platoon. We started with one hundred and eighty soldiers in our company and finished this phase with only forty-three men left alive. Those who remained were all battle-proven soldiers. If an infantryman lasted past the first two weeks of combat, he had a better chance of making it through the war alive.

After we crossed the Siegfried Line, resistance was pretty light. Our orders were to mop up

From The Bronx to Berchtesgaden

On the lookout for German snipers. Photo: National Archives.

through the rubble and round up prisoners. Mostly the prisoners consisted of young boys between fourteen and sixteen, women, and older men. Then we continued to march on.

We had just taken a farm town. My squad was spread out on the kitchen floor of an abandoned house, eating C-rations. We were all tired and filthy. Then there was a knock at the door. Someone entered and yelled, "Attention!" We were so beat that if a general had walked in, no one would have jumped. It turned out to be a first lieutenant in a nice, fresh, clean uniform. The lieutenant stood on top of the

Germany

kitchen table and told us to gather around.

"I know you won't remember my name," he said, and handed out cards with his name on them so that we would remember it. He then proceeded to give us a pep talk reminding us that we were there to kill the Boche. He also told us we would have to shape up and do things according to the GI Manual. We all laughed and went back to what we were doing before he arrived. He did not realize that the average life expectancy for an officer in our outfit was less than two weeks.

I used to write home that I was still in Ordinance, attached to the Infantry. I didn't want my folks to think I was in danger on the front line. One day I received a letter from home saying that they knew I was in the Infantry. Mrs. Rosen, a friend of my mother, told them that her son, Seymour, was in my company. They were hoping that I would take care of him. I was twenty-one years old and he was eighteen. So now I had both Seymour and this new lieutenant to look after. Neither one of them had much battle experience.

That evening our platoon was scheduled to collect prisoners. It was our job to scout around and

From The Bronx to Berchtesgaden

find where the enemy was in force. We would report to headquarters and then the division would move up. When we got the word to move out, I looked at the new lieutenant. I wasn't impressed. The boys were already fatigued and were not happy to go. The radio was not working and could not be repaired. But the lieutenant still ordered us to head out. We were going to cover twelve miles without a radio. We started out late at night after a full day of combat with only a couple hours of rest.

Going on night patrol behind enemy lines to capture prisoners and find out their strength was one of the most hated jobs an infantry soldier could be asked to perform. Shooting enemies was one thing but capturing them was another. Even worse was returning from patrol. Then you had to worry that a frightened, trigger-happy soldier might have forgotten the password and start shooting at *you*.

Our lieutenant, having little combat experience, had us going over hills instead of around them, leaving us vulnerable to enemy gunfire. After a while he said to me, "Okay, sergeant, take over." Our forward observer spotted a farmhouse before which was a truck loaded with ten enemy soldiers.

Germany

We captured them and then surrounded the farmhouse. Inside we found four more German soldiers, who were eager to surrender. Later we found two more soldiers wandering in the woods. As soon as they saw us, they dropped their weapons and came towards us with raised hands.

A little later on we encountered an enemy soldier waving a white flag. One of our new replacements, anxious to take a prisoner by himself, went out alone to round him up. Any experienced infantryman would have known better than to do that. The German soldier with the flag dropped to the ground. His buddies were hiding behind him. They shot and killed our man. After that incident it was payback time. The rest of the way we did not take prisoners. When we saw German uniforms, we fired.

After covering another seven miles, I was staggering from exhaustion. The other soldiers were exhausted, too, and we were all stumbling forward like men in a trance. We had to stop. I posted two guards and we went to sleep in different houses along the route. I was awakened by a Russian boy, whom we had liberated from a forced labor gang. He told us the Boche were coming. I grabbed my Tommy gun and ran out into the street. The Germans saw us, killed the two guards I had posted, and retreated.

The Russian boy asked me if he could stay with us. He was carrying a German machine gun. I explained to him that as much as we would like to have him fight with us, the Army could not take responsibility for him. We could not pay him or draw equipment for him. This refusal, however, did not faze the Russian lad. All he wanted to do was to kill Germans. So the men outfitted him in a GI uniform and made sure he had enough to eat and we allowed him to join our patrol. Not only did he prove himself as a good scout, he was also a great forager and supplied us with fresh eggs. He later joined a group of liberated Russians.

Soon artillery shells started coming our way. At this point our unit was supposed to pull back. I wouldn't move until I found Seymour Rosen, who was asleep in one of the houses.

When we found him, shells were coming in fast, so we started our retreat. We had gone back four miles when we came to a house that looked like a fortress. The door was thick and we couldn't open it. There was a window ten feet up in the wall.

Germany

Sy Rosen was a skinny fellow, being 6' 2" tall but weighing only 145 pounds. So we boosted him up and he crawled through the small window. After five minutes Rosen opened the door. His face was all bloody and beat up. The place was a nunnery and the nuns had thought we were coming to rape them. They calmed down after learning we had no intention of doing so. I sent a messenger back to headquarters and division soon came to relieve us.

We hadn't slept in two days. After the patrol I was so exhausted I lay down in a foxhole and fell sound asleep. A shell landed close to me and still did not wake me. A member of my squad was killed and it still didn't wake me. When I finally opened my eyes, I learned that our new lieutenant had been sent back to the rear with combat fatigue. After only two days of battle he had become so stressed out that his face was distorted and he couldn't move his right arm.

Operation Krautbuster

Operation Krautbuster began behind a furious screen of shells, enabling us to move down the steep banks of the canal and paddle across. We engaged some enemy in a fire fight but they didn't put up much resistance. Among those captured was an SS trooper. To me, all SS troopers seemed ten feet tall but I am sure this man was really no more than six feet. In his belt was a fancy SS dagger.

In my best Yiddish, which sounded like German, I told him to remove the belt and drop it to the ground. He refused, so I knocked him down with my carbine. When he got up, I ordered him again to take it off. He again refused, so I put him down a second time. When he got up for the third time, he pulled the dagger out of

From The Bronx to Berchtesgaden

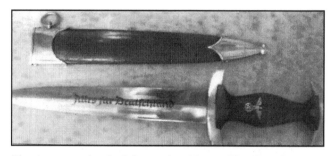

The dagger with which I was sliced by an SS officer. Photo: Murray Soskil.

its sheath and sliced me, cutting my uniform and my stomach. I fired my carbine. Then there was one less German for us to guard.

In the next town we met tough resistance. We were receiving fire and the Germans were moving forward. The company to the right of us was receiving fire. There was a large volume of small arms, artillery, and mortar fire, not only on our right but coming in our immediate direction. The captain got a little anxious, so he told me to take a patrol out to the front and see what was going on. I rounded up a couple of men and we went out a few hundred yards. We got into concealed positions and waited a half hour. Nothing seemed to be happening so the captain ordered us to move forward. But when we attacked, we learned that the Germans had armor

Operation Krautbuster

that we hadn't seen during our scouting, and we ran into fire from thirty-seven flak cannon.

Finally we received support from some Sherman tanks plus our own artillery and the Germans withdrew. Our artillery caught the retreating enemy in a devastating barrage. However, they reorganized and counterattacked, hitting us with artillery, mortars, and machine-gun fire. We were stopped cold. We called for our artillery, which came in shooting once again, and we finally got the upper hand.

Our battalion launched a counterattack and drove the enemy back with heavy losses on both sides. By the end of the day we had bypassed the enemy pill boxes and trenches. As we pushed forward, the enemy kept counterattacking, but we beat them back each time. From the prisoners we took we learned that they had been told by their officers, "Not to worry as the Fuhrer had a master plan and visions for the future."

As we crashed through town after town, strange sights greeted us. Panties, bed sheets, nightgowns—anything that was white—flew from windows that for years had displayed the Nazi swastika. As in France, people lined the streets to stare

From The Bronx to Berchtesgaden

Taking cover under fire in Germany. Photo: Department of Defense.

at us, some out of curiosity and some to glare in open hostility.

In the main street of one of the towns there was a small figure planted in the ground in front of a ruined church. It was a reproduction of Christ crucified, with the head missing. The Nazis did things like this to show their hatred of all religions other then their own.

The church had a high steeple, which the Germans had employed as an observation post. As the church was now empty, I decided to see if there was anything we would be able to use. In one of the panels I found a stack of candles and a few bottles of wine,

Operation Krautbuster

which I passed around the squad. No one objected even though they knew it was communion wine.

Our next objective was the city of Kaiserlautern. Here we encountered especially stiff resistance. Before we were able to go further we had to clean out a complex of apartment buildings that had housed leaders of the Nazi Party, German officers, and French collaborators. These big wigs had departed in such haste that they left behind their belongings and we discovered closets full of expensive women's clothes, furs, and valuable collectibles. Unfortunately, only officers were permitted to collect civilian souvenirs.

We continued on at a fast pace, taking a few more prisoners, who were relieved to be in our company rather than fighting against us since they had been conscripted unwillingly into the German army from many different countries. Then we smelled a strange odor. One of the prisoners told us that there was a concentration camp ahead. As we got closer, the stench became overwhelmingly foul. Then we came upon a high wall made of wire and brick topped with barbed wire.

Beyond the wall the dead bodies of men, women, and children, many naked, were just lying there under the open sky. Piles of bodies were lined up against a wall. These bodies had been used for target practice.

Hanging from the fences were humans who looked like skeletons. They might have weighed eighty or ninety pounds and they were the color of ghosts. We wanted to feed them but we weren't allowed to give them food until the medics had examined them since eating too quickly after a period of starvation will kill a man. One of the live skeletons shuffled up to me and touched me to see if I was real.

"American soldier?" he asked.

"Yes," I said. Then I told him I was Jewish. He started to cry and so did I. He cried without tears, me with tears.

The SS had planned to blow the camp up when it was evacuated but we had advanced so quickly that they hadn't had time to do so and the place was intact.

There was a washroom that spewed gas, not water. There was a row of crematoriums with their own furnaces and huge fans to stoke the fires. There were open graves with hundreds of nude bodies piled in them. Blood was still running in the gutters.

Operation Krautbuster

Inmates of a concentration camp. Photo: National Archives.

There was a large building that was supposed to be a hospital only it was not a place of healing but a place of death. Inside the hospital were filthy rooms in which lay dozens of dead men and women. There were steel tables on which lay cut-open bodies, their internal organs hanging out. There were labs, in each of which were conducted different experiments. Shelves contained jars of human organs and bundles of bone from all parts of the human body. There were human skins stretched on wire. The doctors who had carried out these hideous experiments had left their instruments behind. Their medical certificates were

From The Bronx to Berchtesgaden

A German girl is overcome as she walks past the exhumed bodies of slave workers murdered by SS guards.
Photo: National Archives.

still hanging on the walls of the operating rooms.

I vomited, as did many others. I had killed men and I had seen many men killed and wounded, but to see this inhuman mass atrocity left me in total shock. Most of us thought that if we had come upon this place earlier, we would have killed any German who crossed our path.

We forced the citizens of Kaiserlautern to tour the camp. Although none of them would admit to knowing anything about it, we ordered them to clean up the place, to cover the graves, to wash

Operation Krautbuster

the shelves of the awful laboratories, and to bury the dead with dignity.

It was December of 1944 and the temperature during the day was ten degrees Fahrenheit. At night it was much colder. As the company pushed on deeper into Germany, we had to ford streams, fight, and sleep with constant exposure to low temperature. In order to get the supply personnel to bring us food, hot coffee, and dry socks, we had to threaten them with bodily harm. The cold was so intense I didn't think I would survive. It was so hard to breath that our lungs ached. It was so cold, oil in the engines froze. To get them working, you had to urinate on them and then make sure you closed your pants fast. It seemed as though the nights lasted forever. If a tank was close by, I would huddle by it and try to warm up in its exhaust. By the time dawn arrived, a good portion of the company had frostbite.

There was little sun. It was both raining and snowing. During the day the rain turned the snow into slush and at night the slush froze again. The roads were barely passable. Consequently, the insulated boots, woolen helmet lining, and gloves that were meant for the front lines never reached us. The rear echelons kept these supplies for themselves.

There were more casualties from trench foot than from anything else. We were told to change our socks every day and to massage our feet. But we could rarely get new socks. Nor was it always possible to stick your feet out to massage them. Forty-five thousand men had to be pulled out of the front lines due to trench foot.

One day it rained so hard our foxholes filled with water. It was like sitting in a bathtub, except the water was freezing. We used our helmets to bail out the water. We used our helmets for everything, not just to protect our heads. Often we washed and shaved in them and used them to cook in. Sometimes we even used our helmets as latrines.

There was a fortified farmhouse nearby held by the Germans. Under ordinary circumstances we would not have thought of attacking it but in our desperation to get out of the cold, my squad and I decided to go for it. We had just lost our lieutenant and I was the highest ranking noncom. At my signal we crouched low and started for the house using what shelter we could find. We rushed in with our rifles blazing and machine guns crackling.

Operation Krautbuster

Men fell around me, but after a few grenades were thrown through the windows, all became quiet. No prisoners were taken on either side.

We paid a heavy price for the farmhouse. A portion of my squad was missing. But the rest of us felt it was better to lose a few men than for all of us to freeze to death.

As we were sitting around trying to relax, and finally opening cans of rations, I heard loud voices in the next room. One of our older men was arguing with a new replacement. As I got up to investigate, a shot rang out. The replacement had shot himself in the toe. He had found his own way out of hell. Here was a healthy young man from Boston who had succumbed to battle fatigue. Everyone has a breaking point and this young soldier had reached his. This was not an isolated case.

You can see movies about war or read books about it but only by personal experience can you really know what an infantryman goes through. No one can know what their breaking point is until they reach it. What kept me going were thoughts of home and of my loved ones waiting for me.

The constant turnover of riflemen meant that

From The Bronx to Berchtesgaden

Building defensive works in the snow. Photo: Department of Defense.

my company was now full of ill-trained draftees. Few had volunteered for the Infantry. Most were soldiers with advanced skills who had been given M1 rifles and shunted from safe assignments to the front lines. Many went into combat without having previously fired a weapon. Officers and noncoms who had never been in battle were being given combat assignments.

We found one of our soldiers hiding in a pile of blankets, refusing to fight. No matter what we said to him or how we threatened him, he would not budge. Finally we sent him to the rear to be

Operation Krautbuster

treated for combat fatigue. After two weeks he returned to the company, fit and ready to do his part. As we were advancing, he charged a machine-gun nest and fell on a live grenade to save some buddies. Was it shame or pride that drove him to do this? Was it a desire to redeem himself? Or did he lose his mind? To this day I do not know.

I spent New Year's Eve in a foxhole in the Vosges Mountains. No drinks, no hot food, just our C-rations. Come nightfall, we started digging foxholes. Digging foxholes in freezing weather was not a simple task. We were exhausted before we started. Digging caused you to perspire and with the wind and freezing cold temperatures, the sweat froze and made you feel worse.

There were two men to a hole. Each man took turns watching out for the enemy or catching some Zs. Looking out into the darkness, hearing all kind of frightening sounds, was nerve-racking. Two hours on watch and two hours of sleep did not allow you much rest. After a strenuous day of fighting, you always had to resist falling asleep on guard duty because falling asleep on guard duty was the most serious offense in the Army. For New Years' Eve our artillery gave

From The Bronx to Berchtesgaden

the enemy a tremendous bombardment. As it came down, we started another push forward.

We had not gone far when night set in and once again we started digging foxholes. It was snowing and freezing cold. We spent the night hugging one another to keep warm. We tucked newspapers under our uniforms to insulate our bodies and keep out the wind, and we put leaves on top of us to act as blankets.

Looking up from the foxhole at night after the snow stopped, I saw a full moon and a sky filled with stars. It warmed me a little to know that this same sky was looking down over my loved ones, and my mind kept drifting homeward. I pictured what Pearl might be doing at that exact moment in Connecticut, getting ready for work, having breakfast, writing a letter, or sleeping in a nice cozy bed. Even so I had a hard time sleeping myself. My clothes were wet and I was shivering and shaking with cold.

My foxhole buddy was eighteen years old. He had worked as a delivery boy before the war and dreamed of becoming a supermarket manager when he returned home. Everyone had thoughts of home and pondered their futures, although for many of them there would be no future at all.

Operation Krautbuster

We already had quite a lot of snow but at night we got a little more to add to our misery. In the foxhole we got little uninterrupted sleep because of the threat of enemy patrols sneaking up on us. Every sound made us jumpy. Strange noises and imaginary shadows added to our fears. There was no smoking or talking allowed because sound and light traveled quite a distance.

As we lay there freezing, we were startled by the noise of our own booby traps exploding. For the rest of the night we held our weapons at the ready, expecting an attack. In the morning, however, to our relief we discovered it had been a false alarm. Rabbits had triggered the traps and their dead bodies lay sprawled on the ground, frozen fragments of flesh and fur.

An enemy truck with a loudspeaker began broadcasting treasonous propaganda toward us in English, interspersing their subversive lies with popular American hillbilly music. Our artillery answered with well-placed fire. That silenced the music. Then the Germans started raising white flags pinned to the muzzles of their rifles. They waved their hands in the air and shouted, "*Kamerad*!" When our soldiers went to round them up, the Germans fell flat on the

From The Bronx to Berchtesgaden

ground and other soldiers concealed behind them opened up on our boys. We lost many men to this ruse before we learned the hard way to watch out for the enemy's treachery and to shoot first.

Looking out on an open field, we saw trees that hadn't been there the day before. We studied the field for some time to make sure and eventually we saw movement around the trees. We wired back to a battery of our 105mm guns. They fired several rounds, which exploded all around the German position. Within an hour the place was deserted, trees and all.

When the skies cleared, American fighter-bombers cruising above the clouds spotted the melee below. They came zooming down with cannons and machine guns blazing and the enemy fled.

We were once again moving forward at a brisk pace. Although they were upright and walking, most of the men were practically sound asleep. Exhaustion had taken a dreadful toll on us. Our soldiers were simply going through the motions. Some collapsed, falling to the side of the road. If they had not been picked up, they would have died of exposure. Many had reached their physical and mental limits.

Losses were mounting steadily and it wasn't

Operation Krautbuster

only from enemy fire. Many men were suffering from combat fatigue. They refused to fight and many fled. Others got out of front-line duty by throwing away their false teeth since a man couldn't fight if he couldn't eat. Some exposed their feet to the winter weather to get trench foot. Others shot off their toes in order to get out of the battle. Our feeling of hopelessness cannot be described. We were fighting without promise of either reward or relief. Behind every river there was always another hill—and behind that hill was another river. After weeks or months in the line, only being wounded offered a weary soldier the comfort of safety, shelter, and a bed. Those who were left behind to fight, fought on. We all knew, however, that sooner or later, unless victory came, our journey would end on the medical litter or in the grave.

We then moved to the Frankenthal area in preparation for crossing the Rhine. To get there we had to ford the Moselle River, which was flooded. We crossed in shoulder-deep water. As we were battling the currents, trying to keep our balance with our weapons held high above our heads, German snipers were laying down fire on us. Many men died in those icy waters. Then our artillery opened up and explosions blossomed on the shore and the Germans disappeared, leaving behind their dead and dying.

After the crossing, we were ordered to attack. Ahead of us was rugged terrain with trees and plenty of snow. We were going to climb up and down steep hills. What made it worse was that as the snow was trodden down, it turned to ice, which made the going even more difficult. Furthermore, the Germans had laid down mines with trip sensors, which caused a number of casualties.

Soon enemy artillery fire stopped our advance. We drew together and formed a defensive perimeter. We heard the screams and the cries of the wounded. Our causalities were so heavy that the medics and stretcher-bearers could not keep up with the dead and the wounded. Those that were left behind froze to death. Later we found out that our objective had been taken by another division and our casualties were for naught.

As we continued toward the Rhine, both sides of the road were covered by trees and we could not see far ahead. We heard the sound of a burp gun and then the response of BAR and M1 rifles. The captain or-

Operation Krautbuster

dered six of us to go scout ahead of the company. Two of us had M1 rifles and four had carbines. We saw a group of men coming out of the woods three hundred yards ahead of us. At first we were not sure what side they were on, but after closer inspection, we were able to distinguish their helmets.

I checked the clip in my rifle and put a few additional clips next to me. Then I yelled, "Open fire!" The four soldiers with carbines could not reach the target but my first shot with my M1 took care of a German carrying a machine gun. Together with the man with the other M1, we then took out ten more Germans and the rest decided to surrender.

The Rhine

When we reached Frankenthal, we practiced boat drills and made preparations for crossing the Rhine. Shortly after dusk engineers began bringing boats to the waterfront. There were to be ten of us in a boat. Because of high dikes it was necessary for us to carry the boats by hand to the water's edge. Before we got to the water, enemy mortars had already hit several of the boats. Then an enemy incendiary shell hit a nearby barn, setting it on fire. Soon the area was as bright as day. We were easy targets. Mortar shells kept dropping into the boats. The Germans opened up with small arms fire, machine guns, and artillery. Many men died.

The captain blew a whistle and we ran down the embankment, grabbed the boats by the gun-

From The Bronx to Berchtesgaden

Crossing the Rhine. Photo: National Archives.

wales, and dashed for the river.

All hell broke loose. Lead flew at us from all directions.

Sixteen boats were spread out along a hundred yards of river bank. Some were in shallow water, making it necessary to wade in the mud before we could get into the boats and shove off. The boat I was assigned to was in deep water and I had a hard time climbing aboard with my equipment strapped on my back. An engineer tried to start the motor but it sputtered and died. Luckily, there were oars. Some men used their rifle butts to paddle while

The Rhine

others bailed water with their helmets. We were receiving machine-gun fire and mortar shells were dropping around us. Many boats had holes in their sides and water kept leaking in. Of the sixteen boats we started with, only six reached the far bank.

Dozens of men were in the water. We tried to reach them but our boat kept spinning around and we couldn't get to them. The current was strong and we had a hard time keeping the boat headed toward the opposite shore. When we finally neared the bank, the boat next to mine was hit and everyone was gone. Another boat was unable to navigate the current and floated down the river.

I jumped into the shallow water and waded ashore. There was no time to reorganize. It was every man for himself as we ran forward, firing from our hips. We were charging so fast that the Germans retreated. But we had so few men left that we soon had to halt our advance. We dug our foxholes and waited for supplies and replacements. We had another night to dream of being home in a nice warm bed.

Even though the German infantry withdrew, their artillery seemed to know exactly where we were. At dawn the first shell came booming in, land-

From The Bronx to Berchtesgaden

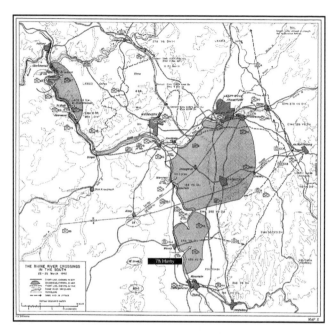

Source: United States Army in World War II, European Theater of Operations, Riviera to the Rhine

ing very close to me, and igniting a streak of light in the semi-darkness. Then larger guns started to pound the forest where we were dug in. The earth rocked and things went flying. Chunks of steel made horrendous noises as they splintered the trees. Wounded men began screaming, yelling for medics, begging for help. The Germans really had us zeroed in.

I jumped out of my foxhole and yelled for everyone to move back. If we had not moved, we would

The Rhine

have been blown to bits. The Germans were using a technique called Time On Target (TOT), which was the military co-ordination of artillery fire by many weapons so that all the munitions arrived at the target at precisely the same time. They were firing Screaming Meemies, which were mortar shells that delivered high explosives with a constant heart-stalling screech. The bombardment was so fierce and relentless that a couple of our soldiers lost control of their bodies.

After the bombardment ended, I discovered a soldier still in his foxhole. He was sobbing and kept digging in the ground with his fingers. I coaxed him out and finally got everyone running forward. We were met by rifle and machine-gun fire, which ironically came from the same foxholes we had just abandoned.

Enemy in white winter combat uniforms surrounded us. Almost half of my men were already lost. I realized our only option was to play dead. I gave the order. We lay there for what seemed like hours although only minutes actually passed before we heard the sound of our own guns coming forward. I raised my head and saw a wounded soldier lying next to me. I took hold of him and dragged him with me as I crawled for the woods. There were some medics with a jeep and they got him back to the battalion aid station still alive. I later found out he made it back to the States.

Then we came to another river. We had all thought we were in the Army, not the Navy, but once again we were to use boats to cross a river. Thankfully, this river was a lot calmer than the Rhine. Since we already had practice handling boats, we knew exactly what to do. We picked up the boats and ran to the water, shoved them in, and climbed aboard. More boats were hit and some capsized. Our motor sputtered and died so we paddled frantically through the smoky haze to the far shore.

At this point we were relieved by another division. We were given a day of rest and received our mail and rations. The cigarette rations were Chelseas or Raleighs—not the first choice of most of the men, who preferred other brands. But the truck drivers were stealing the Lucky Strikes that were supposed to go us, as well as candy bars and other small luxuries. We were fortunate to get the C rations. But the mail was the important thing. Hearing from our loved ones gave us the incentive to stay alive.

One of the older replacements was a guy by

The Rhine

the name of Goran. He was a loner yet we'd had a few conversations together since we both were from New York City. One day the sergeant delivering mail came to me and said he had some bad news for Goran from the Red Cross. His brother had been killed. Since I was the only person Goran was even a bit friendly with, the sergeant thought I should break the news to him. I motioned for Goran to follow me. When we were alone, I said:

"Your brother has been killed."

Goran did not reply. He was silent as we walked back to the other men. Then he turned to me.

"Sarge," he said, "we will make them pay for it tomorrow." After another moment he continued, "You and Bert were all I had, and now he's gone, but I still have you. "

His words got to me. We had fought side by side together and witnessed much death and destruction together. I had not thought that we were friends but now I realized that we were.

One of the hillbillies, who did not know how to write, asked me to write a letter for him to his girlfriend. I flowered up his thoughts a little, for which he was grateful.

From The Bronx to Berchtesgaden

Fighting in Germany. Photo: National Archives.

In the center of town we came across a bank. We blasted open the vault and found stacks of Reichsmark notes. Thinking they were worthless, we used them to start fires. Only afterward did we learn that the notes were negotiable. We all felt sick, thinking of the millions of dollars that had gone up in smoke.

After receiving new replacements, we were on the move again. We were ordered into Ducks (DUKW amphibious assault craft) and crossed the Marne River for the third time. As we reached the other side, civilian snipers targeted us. Anyone shooting at us was fair game so we killed them.

The Rhine

Each batch of replacements seemed younger and cockier than the batch before. One of our older veterans, who must have been all of twenty-two years old, called out to them and asked, "Did you bring your mother along?" Most came into the company not knowing anyone. They were alone and disoriented. They were dumped into combat without knowing what to expect or what was expected from them. Most had not fired more than a few rounds from their rifles before. Many died before they had a chance to get acquainted with the rest of the troops. One new replacement said that he hoped the war wouldn't end until he had a chance to get at the Germans. Another said he would quit the Army and go home the first time he was shot at. They were both wrong. There was still plenty of fighting to be done, and the only way to go home was in a box or with a "million dollar" wound—a wound severe enough to get you sent back to the States, but not bad enough to disable you permanently.

One replacement had lost his buddy, with whom he had been together from the replacement depot. He came over to me and said, "I guess you also must have lost some of your bud-

From The Bronx to Berchtesgaden

dies since you came in."

I replied, "All the soldiers who were here when I came in are gone except for the supply sergeant. Most who came after me are gone, too. That makes me pretty jittery. I keep thinking about the law of averages."

People often said that there were no atheists in foxholes. This was only partly correct. With machine-gun bullets flying in all directions and mortar shells exploding all around you, everyone asked God to look out for them. When you got out of the foxhole, however, and saw all the dead and wounded, you wondered if there was someone watching after all. If there was a God, why were these young men dying and suffering. Most had done nothing wrong in their lives to deserve to be so punished.

As for myself, I knew my wife and family were looking out for me. When I was at my wit's end, I would call out to them and I knew they were praying for me. I am sure that was why I came through the war alive.

The oldest man in our platoon was thirty-two years old. We called him *Pop*. As we approached the city, the Germans made a last-ditch stand. They

The Rhine

started a barrage and the first shell caught Pop in the arm and he received a million-dollar wound, enough to get him a pass home. He was a lucky man.

With our replacements we received a Lieutenant West to lead our platoon. He was originally with the 3rd Infantry Division from another company. He was wounded in the landing in France but he had healed and was sent back to the fighting.

This night we again passed through the enemy trenches in the darkness. All was still. All was quiet. It was too quiet. Suddenly, in the light of the waning moon, we were ambushed. The enemy forces outnumbered us four to one and they were outfitted with artillery, mortars, and small arms.

Our radio was not working and we could not call for reinforcements. Realizing that the platoon would be wiped out, Lieutenant West ran six hundred yards to the battalion command post through a hail of bullets and secured two light tanks to come to our aid. He climbed upon the hull of the lead tank and guided it into battle. A direct hit struck the tank, turning it into a burning pyre and killing the lieutenant. His death was not in vain. The remainder of the battalion was guided to the action

From The Bronx to Berchtesgaden

by the flames and relieved our embattled squad. West had only returned to combat for a few days and his life had already ended. He was a hero. There were many brave heroes like him. Everyone who fought was a hero.

One of our replacements was a short, fat boy who was given the BAR to carry. Browning Automatics Rifles were heavy guns, which made it hard for him to keep up. Anyone who fell behind was usually hit by sniper fire. So I pushed him, carried his gun, and helped with his ammunition. He made it back safely. After the war, he heard that I was coming to Philadelphia on business. He invited me to his house. When I arrived, I discovered a big sign across the street saying, "Welcome, Murray." There was music and food set up in the street. His mother and the whole neighborhood welcomed me. All his relatives, both men and women, kissed me. I lost contact with him a few years later.

Arbeit Macht Frei

Our next push was to Bad Kessingen, a city known for its fine springs and numerous resort hotels. Twenty of these hotels had been converted into German military hospitals. They had red crosses on the roofs, which saved the city from Allied bombings. None of the houses had sustained any damage. After we took the city, however, the enemy sent planes to bomb it even though there were German soldiers still in the hospitals.

A German soldier who couldn't have been more than fourteen years old appeared, carrying a white flag. He spoke excellent English. He let us know that the garrison wished to surrender. We followed him to the town square, which was filled with German soldiers, who stacked their arms in piles be-

From The Bronx to Berchtesgaden

fore us. Two bodies were hanging from the city hall balcony. They were officials who had wanted to surrender. SS troopers had hung them as traitors.

We came across a factory that manufactured dress suits. The GIs went into the factory and came out wearing high hats and bow ties with their dirty uniforms. Somehow we managed to find a little humor even in war, but we never lost focus on the fact that there was always another push and another objective ahead of us. And so on we went.

The Marne River kept zigzagging, and we had been forced to cross the same stream several times as we advanced into Germany. Now we had to get over it a fourth time. Boats were brought forward and unloaded and then shoved off calmly. Resistance hadn't been expected but suddenly there was a swish and a bunch of flares exploded, bathing the area in bright light. Shells started landing around us. As I reached shore, tracer bullets were zipping over my head. I jumped into a ditch until our own artillery returned fire and blasted the enemy until they retreated.

As we came to the railway yards on the outskirts of Nuremberg, we discovered eight cattle

Arbeit Macht Frei

cars. When we opened the doors, the bodies of GIs tumbled out. The Germans had riddled the boxcars with machine-gun fire. Most of the GIs were dead, but there were some still alive, having been protected by the corpses of their friends. After seeing this atrocity, it was difficult for any of us to maintain our composure, particularly as we had heard how well German POWs were being treated in America. The fellows were angry enough to fire at anyone who moved.

Next we captured the city of Bamberg, a

A young German soldier surrenders. Photo: National Archives.

From The Bronx to Berchtesgaden

German hospital city. The hospitals were large and well equipped and their beds were filled with recuperating German soldiers. Many of them had armless sleeves pinned to their shoulders or wooden crutches to replace missing legs. With utter disregard for the German patients, the Luftwaffe bombed the area, hitting the hospitals and making casualties of their own men.

Continuing from Bamberg we discovered another concentration camp. This was a work camp, not an extermination camp, although there was re-

Civilians join together in Bamberg, Germany to rescue a building's contents and put down a fire caused by a Luftwaffe raid. Photo: National Archives.

Arbeit Macht Frei

ally little difference between the two since the ultimate purpose of both was to exterminate their occupants. The prisoners in their striped pajamas were little more than skeletons. Their eyes were sunk into their skulls and they appeared to be sightless. A tall barbed-wire fence topped by electrocution boxes encompassed the entire camp. There was a big sign reading, *"Arbeit Macht Frei"*—work makes you free. The stench of decaying flesh was overpowering. There must have been five thousand people in a space meant to hold four hundred. The buildings were without doors or windows to keep the cold out. Many of the prisoners were sick with dysentery and typhus. They shuffled over to beg for crumbs, but again we could not oblige them. The doctors and medics would have to attend to them first.

Near the administration building was a cluster of huts housing the ovens. The fires were still burning and blood was still running in the gutters. In back of these houses were open graves containing hundreds of naked corpses twisted in death. We also found a few bodies of German guards. They were mostly old men who had been left behind while the elite made a hasty retreat. They had

From The Bronx to Berchtesgaden

Burned out German tank. Photo: National Archives.

been beaten to death by the inmates.

General Eisenhower decreed that the remaining bodies be buried in public places and maintained with perpetual care and that crosses and Stars of David should be placed at the head of each grave. We rounded up the townspeople and ordered them to dig holes six feet deep. The entire population was required to attend the burial services.

As we continued on, we ran into a new German defensive line. The enemy had tanks, roadblocks, and mine fields. My squad was waiting in a bombed-out house when we saw a German Tiger tank coming down the street. It stopped to allow the German infantry to clear some mines before it

Arbeit Macht Frei

went any further.

One soldier in my squad hurled a grenade into the mine field. This caused a chain reaction. Mine after mine blew up, making the street look like Fourth of July fireworks. Many Germans were blown to pieces. Then an antitank shell struck the lead tank and the Tiger burst into flames. The men trapped inside began screaming but soon they became quiet. The surviving Panzers started pulling back. Their infantry also began retreating.

Although there were only a few men left in our squad, we ran forward. One soldier carried the machine gun, one carried the ammunition, and I carried the tripod. Bending low to the ground, we trotted forward with our burdens and then we dropped flat as shells kept popping all around us. There was nothing we could do but pray while the earth shook. Then we heard the booming of American artillery coming from the rear, so we picked ourselves up and started moving forward again.

We saw a perfect spot for the machine gun. There were some logs for cover and a perfect field of view. My squad wanted to set up in that spot but I held them back. I didn't know why myself. I just

From The Bronx to Berchtesgaden

3rd Division patrol in Nuremberg. Photo: Department of Defense.

knew. It was as though I had a sixth sense. Another machine gun team took the spot. A few seconds later there was a flash and a direct hit on the position we had almost taken up. All three men from the other squad were torn apart. Then the company moved ahead in small rushes until nightfall, when we were ordered to attack. Heavy artillery and machine-gun fire met our rush forward. The German counterattack almost drove our battalion back but our massive firepower slaughtered them instead. Then the battalion swept forward.

On April 13th we got word that President

Arbeit Macht Frei

Roosevelt had died. We were shocked but we knew the war would go on as before. General Eisenhower ordered every available soldier to attend a memorial service in the president's honor.

The Germans were determined to make a strong defense of Nuremberg, which was a Nazi shrine. Approaching the city, we came under fire from hundreds of antiaircraft guns being employed as artillery, firing horizontally instead of skyward. We were opposed by three battle groups—air force personnel, men from the officer's candidate school, and the Nuremberg police department. They were armed with pistols, rifles, and *panzerfaust*—disposable preloaded launch tubes firing high explosive anti-tank warheads. Hundreds of snipers were concealed in the debris. The Germans used every trick in the book to hold the city. Mines and booby traps all combined to make our attack costly. Worse, the German air force was still flying overhead, dropping antipersonnel bombs on us.

My squad was hiding in the woods on the outskirts of the city. In front of us was an open field covered by machine gun crossfire, which was protecting a minefield. We also heard small arms fire in the near

From The Bronx to Berchtesgaden

distance. We could not use grenades for fear of hitting the branches above us and having shrapnel fall on us. Then our own artillery opened up and we were able to move ahead in small dashes.

Penetrating Nuremberg was made doubly difficult by the fact that it was a city within a city. There was a wall surrounding the inner section, which was once the fortified Nuremberg of feudal days. SS Panzers and grenadiers held on for three days before finally retreating behind the ten-foot-thick walls of the old city. Our howitzers, placed five hundred yards from the wall, could only nick the outer plaster.

It was up to the infantry to scale the walls, rush the two gates, and probe our way through pitch-black narrow passageways. We had just cleared a house when we heard the sound of a tank motor and saw quite a few German infantrymen coming forward, accompanying the Panzer. We kept firing at the infantry and the turret of the tank. It was almost pointed directly at us when we saw a flash and a ball of fire hit the underbelly of the tank. There was a huge explosion and the machine burst into flames. The soldiers inside did not

Arbeit Macht Frei

Searching for snipers. Photo: Department of Defense.

have a chance to get out. We let out a cheer.

Then another tank came at us. Our bazooka man arrived with his weapon and we concealed ourselves in ambush. I loaded the rocket just as the tank passed. The corporal pressed the trigger of the bazooka. Nothing happened. Quickly I undid the connection and scraped the connecting wire. The tank began backing up. This time the bazooka fired and the cor-

From The Bronx to Berchtesgaden

German soldiers surrender. Photo: National Archives.

poral put the round squarely into the tank's engine, paralyzing the machine. One of the tankers jumped from the Panzer and was immediately mowed down. My squad took care of the others trying to get away.

Fighting was house-to-house and room-to-room. Finally we reached Adolph Hitler Platz. The Germans kept falling back slowly but soon civilians emerged from cellars, joined the enemy ranks, and began to attack us with picks and shovels. We drove off the townspeople and shot about one hundred enemy soldiers. The entire police force surrendered *en masse*. Nuremburg was ours.

Berchtesgaden

We were issued clean uniforms with ascots and given a little time to wash, shave, and make ourselves presentable. We assembled outside of town in formation for review. A band played marching tunes and we paraded in the Sportplatz. There were many high-ranking brass assembled. Our division commander, General John W. "Iron Mike" O'Daniel, gave a speech.

"Officers and men of the 7th Regiment," he said. "I have great news for you. I know you are bored with this rear-echelon, non-combat duty, so I am pleased to advise you that we are returning to combat."

O'Daniel may have been happy at the idea of returning to combat but few of the troops shared his enthusiasm. There was a lot of grumbling in the

From The Bronx to Berchtesgaden

ranks. Personally, I had no complaints about boredom, nor any great impatience to return to the front lines. Still our great commander continued on in the same vein. War was hell for those who did the killing and the dying. Only those who had never fired a shot or had the enemy firing at them gloried it.

In war you had no winners. Only losers. Those who glorified war dishonored the memory of the young men who suffered and died in combat. I heard my name called out by the general himself. I stepped forward and he pinned a Silver Star on my chest and shook my hand.

We paraded in the Platz after placing an American flag in front of the palace. This occurred on Hitler's birthday. Since Hitler had announced that for a birthday present he wished that every German civilian would kill one American, we were doubly alert and shot at anything that moved.

I set my squad up in a hotel in the center of town. After placing guards, we went to sleep in real beds for the first time in months. We were given a hot meal, clean clothes, and our mail. This reminder of home brought more heartbreak. We also received a copy of the *3rd Infantry Division Front*

Berchtesgaden

Line, a paper reporting news of the division. In it I found my picture along with an explanation of why I had received my Silver Star.

Our division was supposed to go into reserve but unfortunately there was to be no rest for the weary. Word came down from command that a bridge over the Danube River had been captured, clearing the way for an approach to Munich. We were on the move again. As we crossed the bridge, we encountered Tiger tanks armed with 120mm guns. Every five minutes a concentration of fifty guns was fired at us. Our side took some losses but with the help of the Air Force, we recaptured the bridge.

Here we had one of the most joyous and memorable liberations of the war. Fifty-two men of the 3rd Infantry Division, who had been captured in Anzio more than a year before, were set free. They were a sorry-looking lot because of all that they endured and they were overjoyed to see us.

Then we hit a resistance pocket consisting of several hundred *Hitler-Jugend* (Hitler Youth). These were all boys, none more than sixteen years of age.

After a terrific mortar barrage, the *Hitler-Jugend* broke, screaming out, "*Kamerad, Kamerad!*"

From The Bronx to Berchtesgaden

while trying to surrender. They flung away their guns and ran toward our lines. Behind them, however, were SS officers, who had been forcing the boys to fight at gunpoint. They shot the *Hitler-Jugend* in the back, killing six, while we killed those who continued to fight. I felt terrible having to shoot children. But when you're fired upon, the age of your enemy does not matter. You have no other choice.

On the road to Munich we came to the city of Augsburg. The German commander capitulated without putting up resistance and we hardly paused our pursuit of the German army. Marching on foot, we covered twenty-five miles during the first day of our trek. We went down the Munich Autobahn, clearing the suburbs around the city. The last barrier facing us was the Amper River. Of the many bridges spanning the flow, only one remained standing. Crossing it, we were in the city.

After another fierce battle we overcame a force of three hundred German infantry armed with machine guns. Some civilians pointed out the hiding places of enemy troops afraid to surrender. Some civilians even showered us with flowers. But as we worked our way through the streets towards the

Berchtesgaden

THE FRONT LINE

Pfc. MURRAY SOSKIL, Co. G, 7th Inf., Home town—Bronx, N.Y: At Utweiler snipers nearly got me as I attempted to run a message back to obtain support against the counterattacking Kraut tanks cutting us to pieces. I was lucky, in short rushes, to get past a nearby tank on our flank. But soon ran right into six Boche, one with a Burp gun. They were so surprised they surrendered. I was more surprised when I got out of that town, still alive, and with the Kraut as PWs.

From The Bronx to Berchtesgaden

center of the city, we encountered a suicide squad of twenty-five German Elite Guards, who were holding out in a building. They surrendered only after one of our artillery pieces tore the structure down around them.

General Eisenhower ordered a policy of non-fraternization with the conquered populace. This command was not well received by our GIs. Most of our men were young and horny. They hadn't seen a girl or had sex for months. Most dreamed and talked about nothing else. They wanted nothing more than to have a German woman.

Many violated the standing orders against looting. The German officers and collaborators had retreated so fast that they left behind closets filed with coats, silverware, and fine paintings. Everyone, myself included, picked out things to send home. Unfortunately, the officers who examined our packages confiscated these items for themselves.

The war was now coming to an end. Our entire military apparatus was rushing forward in armored columns, trucks, and jeeps. The infantry still had a few pockets of resistance to clean up but the Germans were giving up by the thousands. Some

Berchtesgaden

had their families with them. We didn't even bother to take them prisoner but just sent them to the rear and continued our march.

The fighting let up and a few days later we crossed the Saalach River in assault boats. We faced no opposition. We had the honor of being the first troops to enter Austria. The German collapse was almost complete. Over three thousand prisoners

Hitler's private retreat. Photo: Murray Soskil.

From The Bronx to Berchtesgaden

were taken, among them three generals.

Our next objective was Hitler's private retreat in the Bavarian mountain town of Berchtesgarden, which was known as *Adlerhorst* (Eagle's Nest) and was at an elevation of eight thousand feet. To make the place easy for Hitler to reach, German engineers had constructed an elevator shaft that ran from the base of the mountain all the way to the top.

Adlerhorst was something from a storybook. The Air Force had done a thorough job in bombing the place but even so most of the structure was still intact. With a little imagination you could tell how magnificent it must have been. The villa contained a large picture window from which you could see parts of Germany and the city of Saltzburg in Austria. The walls of Hitler's study were lined with bookshelves. Dust coated everything. The guys went through Hitler's clothes and his desks, taking whatever souvenirs they could conceal. That afternoon we placed an American flag over the charred buildings.

The television series *Band of Brothers* gave credit to the paratroopers of the 101st Airborne for capturing Berchtesgarden. This was incorrect. The 3rd Infantry Division was there first. My bud-

Berchtesgaden

dy Seymour Rosen wrote to the producers of the show, informing them of the error they had made. He received a letter of apology but little could be done to change what was already recorded.

Still the Germans, who only a short time ago had been so full of fight, continued to come in from the hills like sheep to surrender. Everyone wanted safe entry into a POW cage. The roads to the rear were clogged with surrendering soldiers accompanied by camp followers, men and women of all ages. The civilians were panicky and fearful of what the approaching Russian army would do to them. They

3rd Infantry Division GIs toasting the capture of Hitler's Berghof. Photo: U.S. Army.

From The Bronx to Berchtesgaden

believed that the Russians were barbaric and that their combat soldiers were savages. Considering how poorly the German army had treated the Russian population, their apprehension was not unfounded.

An entire German army of one hundred and fifty thousand men surrendered to an American division of only ten thousand. They came through in reverse order. Army headquarters staff first, then divisions and regiments. Combat troops came through last. The general staff, including ten generals, were in excellent condition. They were shaved and groomed. Their uniforms were clean and their boots were shined. They wore monocles and medals. They rode in large chauffeured cars accompanied by their wives or mistresses. The rear echelon troops were in excellent condition, too, and looked much better than our own combat forces.

Then their fighting men came up. These soldiers were not riding but on foot. They were a dirty, unkempt bunch and their shoes were held together by rags. As the Germans passed our checkpoint, we disarmed them and relieved them of their cameras, watches, and other items. We soldiers collected a few trinkets but the officers confiscated the valu-

Berchtesgaden

German prisoners marching to captivity. Photo: National Archives.

able items for themselves.

We entered the city of Salzburg with ten thousand men and secured the place without casualties.

From The Bronx to Berchtesgaden

American GI drinks his fill. Photo: National Archives.

After stringing up barbed wire enclosures, we had one hundred and fifty thousand prisoners surrendered to us. Some were still carrying their guns.

I was given a small section of the city center to guard. In this area was a champagne warehouse. Our fellows wanted to celebrate the fact that they were still alive. Soon corks were popping everywhere. Each man drank his fill and poured the rest away. No one would consider drinking from the same bottle as another man.

The quartermasters opened a PX where we could buy things inexpensively. Cigarettes were five cents a pack. Candy bars, soap, and toothpaste were three cents. These small luxuries were valuable

Berchtesgaden

commodities in the war-torn city and the GIs used them to trade with the German civilians.

Our billet was a five-story hotel. When I went to inspect the place, I found three or four women in each room with the GIs. They had flocked to Salzberg to seek protection from the approaching Russian army. I sent them away and posted guards on the stairs. But it was tough to keep the men, who had not seen a woman for months, away from the girls. Many fellows indulged themselves despite my best efforts. As for myself, I was a married man and I stayed true to my Pearl.

Eisenhower issued a special order to the Army, stating that every GI, including officers, would need a bill of sale for any civilian item found in their possession. If not, they would be subject to court-martial and punishment. Rape and looting would also be prosecuted to the fullest extent of military law. The GIs were happy to hear that the officers were included in this directive. Everyone started throwing their souvenirs away.

We entered Salzburg on the 3rd of May. Two days later our excess ammunition was taken away from us. This was good since it meant fighting was

From The Bronx to Berchtesgaden

3rd Division GIs in Salzburg.

over. We all thought we were home free. Unfortunately, our ammunition was soon returned to us and we were sent into the Alps, where Field Marshal Kesselring still commanded an intact army. That old feeling of hopelessness returned. The passageways into the Alps were high and narrow. The approach was structured so that a hundred men could hold off a division. Our causalities would be tremendous if we had to attack. As we got to the foothills, however, we were relieved to hear bands playing. Kesselring and his entire army passed right by us on their way to surrender.

Peace

Peace was declared on May 8th, 1945, which also happened to be my birthday. After living in constant fear of death and physical injury for so long, it took time for the fact that the war was over to sink in. After a while, however, as time passed without gunfire, as I filled my belly with good food, and slept at night in a real feather bed without worrying about being murdered in my sleep, I began to accept that peace had come.

A man is changed when he comes to within an inch of death time after time, as I did. To be alive is a miracle I cannot understand. I cannot forget the deaths of the many men who fought beside me. I still ask myself, "Why them and not me?" More than sixty years have passed since the war and still I am haunted

From The Bronx to Berchtesgaden

by my memories of the dead and the maimed.

The 3rd Infantry suffered more casualties than any other division in the U.S. Army—34,227 altogether. The 7th Regiment alone had more than ten thousand casualties. Over 80 percent were riflemen. More than 80 percent of officers killed were

Peace

first and second lieutenants.

More than sixteen million Americans served in the armed forces during the war but fewer than one million saw combat. The Infantry represented just 14 percent of the troops overseas but they bore the brunt of the fighting and suffered seven out of ten of all casualties.

Those who endured the hardships of battle were forever afterward grateful to be alive. The combat we encountered was beyond comprehension. You had to experience it to understand it. Unfortunately, the highest ranking officer you ever saw in combat was your company commander, maybe a captain. The higher ups knew nothing about what fighting was really like. Nor did the enlistees lucky enough to be assigned to rear-echelon duty. They lived a very different life from the front-line troops.

Men on the front line had only each other to depend upon. The best way an infantryman could protect himself overnight was by digging a deep trench to sleep in. There were always two rows of trenches along each side of a road. In the infantry there were round faces and long faces, smooth faces and rough faces, yet they all looked the same. They all had the same expression

From The Bronx to Berchtesgaden

because they had no expression at all.

Our days of fighting in Europe were at an end. After three long hard years of digging foxholes, dodging shells, hiking through ice and snow and intense cold, and seeing our buddies blown to smithereens, we no longer had to fight. For a while there were rumors that our division would be sent to Japan after a rest period, and we all breathed a sigh of relief when we heard that the atom bomb had been dropped and that Japan had surrendered.

Rear-echelon troops relieved us and we were given time to clean ourselves and relax awhile. Then we were issued new uniforms and equipment, transported by truck to the German city of Bieben, and assigned to occupation duty. Our quarters were plush. I couldn't believe I was in the same army in which I had served for so long. There were four men to a room but each room had its own bathroom and shower. We also had a nice dining and recreation hall. These originally had been the billets of German officers.

There were few old timers left among us. The supply sergeant, who had been with the division for two and a half years, had accrued enough points to

Peace

Supply Sergeant Murray Soskil.

be sent home immediately. The point system went by the amount of time you were overseas and not by the danger you were in while you were there. Since I did not have enough points to be sent home, I was given the supply sergeant's job in his place. The position came with a fully-stocked supply room and an

From The Bronx to Berchtesgaden

office of my own. My duty was to keep records and see to it we had all the supplies we needed on hand.

One day I realized there was a tremendous demand for GI soap bars. As we had an army laundry, I knew the GIs were not washing their own clothes. I soon found out the reason for this demand. The German women did not have soap and they would give the GIs special favors for a single bar of the stuff. Even when I cut the soap bars in half, the GIs still received the same favors, so I finally cut the bars in quarters to make the limited supply of soap last longer.

The official occupation currency was the Allied Military Mark. These were printed in Washington and their circulation was strictly controlled. However, duplicate plates were given to the Russians, who printed marks by the millions to pay their occupation troops. Unlike American soldiers, who could convert marks to dollars, Russians could not convert marks into rubles. They carried around briefcases filled with money and tried to buy anything small enough to smuggle back home. Watches were a lucrative item. Even Mickey Mouse watches were at a premium. GIs could get a watch from the PX for

Peace

$16 and sell it to the Russians for $150 to $200. The Germans, too, were bartering their family valuables for cigarettes, coffee, and candy. When they ran out of these items, the women would offer their bodies. There were many takers.

On the outskirts of town was a group of barracks that had been converted into a hospital for German women with venereal disease. Nearby was an Air Force base. The Air Force soldiers would get leave and come into town. They passed the women's barracks and the women in the hospital waved for them to come in. The Air Force men did not know why the ladies were there. They found ways to sneak in to the hospital even though we had guards posted. Soon there was a sorry bunch of Air Force personnel. They stopped sneaking into the place.

The civilian population was cooperative and accepted occupation readily and many came to work for us but no one could be trusted. Fathers informed on their own daughters in order to curry favor with the authorities. No one, however, would admit to being a Nazi or admit to knowing anyone else who had been a Nazi.

From The Bronx to Berchtesgaden

In the sector under Russian control conditions were harsh for the German civilians. The Russians stole everything of value they could find, sending truckload after truckload of loot back to their homeland. Since the Germans had beaten, raped, and murdered Russian women while the country was under German occupation, the Russians were determined to do the same to the German women now that they had the power to do so. Some of my boys were arrested for fighting with Russian soldiers when they saw them molesting German civilians.

After a few weeks of living in luxury, my points came due. Eleven of us were informed that we were to be returned to the States. Since dogface infantrymen are rarely asked for their opinion in the Army, it surprised us all when we were given the choice of taking the northern or the southern route back home We chose the northern route since it was shorter. This was a mistake.

We were sent to the city of Bravenhaven to wait for our ship. Unfortunately, the port was closed due to the many vessels that had been sunk in the harbor. We would have to wait until a passage was cleared. There was not much we could do while we waited

Peace

Murray Soskil in Salzburg.

From The Bronx to Berchtesgaden

but write letters and dream about coming home. It was a boring time, which went on far too long. Occasionally we would have a movie to watch but that was about it. There were no shows or donuts from the Red Cross. In fact, in all the years I was overseas, I hardly saw the Red Cross or received a donut.

Many soldiers broke out in rashes. They had contracted scabies from intimate engagements with infected women. You were not allowed to board a ship if you had scabies. One morning I woke up and my back was itching. I was panic-stricken, afraid that I would be denied passage home even though I had never touched a woman besides my wife while I was in the Army. I told myself that I must have contracted scabies from a dirty blanket or sheets, but I knew no one would believe this story.

I ran directly to the battalion medics. They looked at my back and told me that I indeed had scabies. The only cure for the disease at the time was sulphur. The medics covered my back with sulphur salve. The next day my back was worse, so they lathered more sulphur dressing on. Still my rash worsened.

I went to the hospital. Doctors gave me a few tests. Then they told me to show-

Peace

er off the sulphur from my back. I did not have scabies after all. After three years in the Army, and after all that I had endured, I had become allergic to wool.

They issued me cotton uniforms, called *suntans*, and sent me on my way.

Coming Home

After a month the harbor of Bremerhaven was clear and we were finally homeward-bound. The ship to which we were assigned was not a luxury liner. It was so small it could almost be called a boat. Most troop transport ships were large enough to ride three waves, which made them fairly stable in the water, but this vessel could only ride two waves, so it was going up and down all the time. Worse, we were in the North Atlantic at the height of winter and I was wearing light cotton suntans while everyone else had on warm wool.

The ship held five hundred men. Quarters were crowded and there were two tiers of hammocks. When one hammock swayed, they all swayed. No one ate much because everyone was nauseaus. We could

From The Bronx to Berchtesgaden

not go outside because the decks were being swept by monumental waves. Most of the soldiers and crew kept running to the latrines. The stench of so many seasick men is impossible to describe.

Pearl tracked the progress of my ship on a daily basis. One day the Army told her the ship had actually lost ground due to strong currents and bad weather. The Atlantic crossing was supposed to take seven days but it took eleven.

We arrived in Fort Dix at 11 PM. When I heard that we would not be discharged for another two days, I threw my equipment on the bunk and took off for the gate. An MP stopped me and asked for my pass. I didn't have one, of course, but I told him my story and he in turn told me that there was a hole in the fence a hundred yards down the line. He also let me know when the best time was to return to the base without being noticed.

I took a cab to Trenton and caught a milk train at four o'clock in the morning to New York. I could have run faster than that train, or so it seemed to me. At 6 AM I was in a taxi to Bryant Avenue in The Bronx. Soon afterward I was ringing the doorbell.

No one had been expecting me. Pearl, who

Coming Home

had been staying with my family, answered the door with her hair in curlers. I can not express our joy at being reunited after so long. Unfortunately, after two happy days, I was forced to return to Fort Dix. This, however, was not to be for long. One hour after I got back, they called my name and discharged me. I was in The Bronx in short order and soon resumed my life as a civilian.

Pearl and my mother had been looking around for an apartment to rent for us. Due to all the GIs coming home, there was a shortage of rentals in the city, and the best they could find was a small three-room place on the fifth floor of a walk-up building. The rent was $28 a month, and the apartment was small and hard to reach, but it was our palace. We lived there a year and a half and it was there that my first son, Norman, was born.

I was not sure what I wanted to do with my future. I visited my old boss at the Larsen Importing Company, a watch material supplier. He was happy to see me alive but he did not offer me a job. I thought about going back to school under the GI Bill but I knew I could not do so because I had to support my family. Pearl and I decided to go on a second honey-

From The Bronx to Berchtesgaden

moon before making any decisions. We went to the Laurels Hotel in the Catskill Mountains.

It was wintertime and it was snowing and it was a perfect setting for a honeymoon. We shared a lodge with five other couples. That evening there were several dance contests and every couple won at least one. We were given six bottles of Champagne with which to celebrate as we sat around the fireplace. It was a time never to be forgotten.

Upon returning to the city, I went to see Mr. Larsen again. This time he offered me a position with the company as a salesman. The next day I started my career with LIC. This was to last thirty-five years.

My boss sent out notices to his accounts informing them that his new sales representative would visit them shortly and telling them about my service record and my Silver Stars. I had never been a salesman before but I figured that since I was already familiar with the company merchandise, I would do well at the job if I gave it my best effort.

On my first trip to Boston, however, I was not greeted with open arms. Apparently my boss had not fairly distributed his merchandise among his clients during the war. His entire inventory had gone to the

Coming Home

Murray and Pearl Soskil in Boca Raton. Photo: Brett Soskil.

accounts that had paid him the most money. All I heard were complaints about the firm and no orders came in. I was not encouraged by this reception. Pearl had accompanied me to Boston and during lunch together she told me to try again. So I made the rounds a second time and eventually came away with orders from five out of six accounts.

After three years in our small apartment, we moved into a place with four large rooms in an elevator building. Here our second son, Marvin, was born.

Every Sunday morning, when I would open

From The Bronx to Berchtesgaden

the front door, there would be a bag of bagels sitting on the mat before the apartment. This was a gift from my war buddy, Seymour Rosen, who had started a bagel route. A couple years later he became an audio specialist and settled in Atlanta, Georgia. We kept in touch by phone almost every week and occasionally visited one another. I still called him *kid* and he called me *old man*.

Eventually Pearl and I were able to afford a house in Little Neck, New York, which was a neighborhood at the very end of the borough of Queens. Worrying about the mortgage kept me up at night but we were happy there and soon our third son, Joel, was born, completing our family. This place was to be our home for more than forty years.

One year Pearl was the chairperson of a local charity bazaar. She needed more merchandise for the function than had been donated and she asked me if I could help. A couple of my accounts were jobbers of gift ware. They let me have merchandise at cost, and we sold it at the bazaar for a profit. After the event, we kept getting requests for more of the items that I had purchased from the jobbers. Pearl suggested we should start a

Coming Home

business. Thus was born Little Neck Jewelers.

We did not have enough money to stock an exclusive jewelry store so we had to improvise. Our cabinets and shelving came from kiosks in the World's Fair in Flushing Meadow Park, which was closing. I bought our air conditioning unit at an auction after bribing two other bidders to drop out. There wasn't a toy store in Little Neck, or a stationers, so I sold toys and greeting cards in addition to a small selection of inexpensive jewelry. Gradually, however, as business improved, we dropped all the other items and Little Neck Jewelers became a successful enterprise.

We now live at the Polo Club in Boca Raton, Florida and we think it is paradise. Our family now includes my three sons, Norman, Marvin, and Joel, their wives Joan, Janise, and Carol, seven grandchildren, and ten great-grandchildren.

I am a fortunate man to have come through the war alive and I take pride in what I accomplished, both during battle and afterward. Despite the decades that have passed, however, the horrors of war are still as close to me as yesterday and I cannot keep from thinking of all the fellows who were not so lucky. Many more men deserved recognition

From The Bronx to Berchtesgaden

than actually received it. They were the ordinary and the extraordinary. Most are now gone but they will never be forgotten. They were all heroes.

Once again I repeat:

In your memory, I salute you.

Murray Soskil
3rd Infantry Division, World War II
Served with the 3rd Infantry Division, G Company, 7th Infantry Regiment in the European Theater, including southern France, Germany, and Austria. Battles included Augsburg, Salzburg, Nuremberg, and Munich. He was awarded two Silver Stars, a Bronze Star, the Presidential Unit Citation, six Battle Stars, and a French award for bravery.

Made in the USA
Lexington, KY
29 December 2013